MONEY ROCK$

WARNING

Money may cause you to behave ERRATICALLY, spend EXCESSIVE or act IMPULSIVELY

USE WITH EXTEM KNOWLEDGE & CAU

Second Edition

SUE LYNN SASSER · RANDAL ICE

UNIVERSITY
OF CENTRAL
OKLAHOMA

 KENDALL/HUNT PUBLISHING COMPANY
4050 Westmark Drive   Dubuque, Iowa 52002

CONTENTS

DEAR READER

Talking about money often makes us feel uncomfortable, especially if we are in debt or struggling with our financial situation. Money directly relates to our own childhood experiences and family values, so there is no "one size fits all" formula and no set path for "living' large."

Money Rocks is designed especially for people who live in the 21st century, where we are bombarded with advertising, credit card offers, and zillions of temptations to spend. Yet, most of us have never been taught how to save or plan for our retirement—even though it seems light years away.

Today's consumer has so many more choices to make than in previous generations. We have more career opportunities, greater potential for wealth, greater potential for bankruptcy, greater possibility of being scammed, more places to shop, and more products to buy than ever before.

Learning a few basic skills won't guarantee us fame and fortune. But, in the words of Benjamin Franklin, "Your net worth to the world is usually determined by what remains after your bad habits are subtracted from your good ones."

With this book, our goal is to help you increase your net worth by minimizing those bad financial habits and maximizing the good ones.

May you find meaning in every journey, growth in every challenge, purpose in every action, and self-confidence in every moment of doubt.

Sincerely,

Dr. Sue Lynn Sasser
Dr. Randal Ice

ACKNOWLEDGMENTS

The authors wish to thank Lacy Myers for her editorial and creative assistance with the project, Allen Arnold for his suggestions of topics, and the staff at Kendall Hunt for their help in producing the final product.

AUTHOR BIOGRAPHIES

Sue Lynn Sasser is an associate professor of economics in the College of Business Administration at the University of Central Oklahoma. In addition, she serves as director of the UCO Center for Economic Education, executive director of the Oklahoma Council on Economic Education and past president of the Oklahoma Jump$tart Coalition for Personal Financial Literacy. Dr. Sasser has a PhD in Consumer Economics from Texas Woman's University and is active in the National Association of Economic Educators. She has been involved in developing educational materials for twenty-five years, and is a frequent presenter on economic and personal financial literacy. Dr. Sasser joined the UCO faculty in 2001. She is married with two sons and six grandchildren.

Randal Ice is a professor of finance in the College of Business Administration at the University of Central Oklahoma and has been teaching personal finance for over twenty years. Dr. Ice chairs the Finance Department at UCO and is nationally recognized for his work in personal finance education at the college level. He hosted a weekly radio show for four years on business and education issues in Central Oklahoma and has been widely quoted in the media on financial topics. He currently teaches courses in Personal Finance, Business Finance, Investments, Real Estate, and Financial Statement Analysis. He is married with two sons and four grandchildren. Dr. Ice joined the UCO faculty in 1984 and has a doctorate from Oklahoma State University.

CHAPTER ONE

YOUR FINANCIAL FUTURE

If someone offered you a recording contract, would you make a few recordings and just see what happened? Would you settle for singles that had no hope of getting in the top 40—let alone being number one on the charts? Or, would you strive and strategize to become the next best-selling international sensation? Can you imagine the winner of one of the hottest TV reality shows wanting to be a one-hit wonder? Probably not.

Few of us purposely set out to fail. We have dreams, wishes, hopes, and desires for our lives. Some are practical and easily attainable; others may be a bit idealistic. But each of us has some idea about our "ideal" future, our preferred lifestyle and our sense of purpose—even if we aren't sure how to achieve it.

Our future is full of choices. In fact, we make hundreds of choices each day—what to wear, what to eat, where to go, whom to see, how to react, where to shop, what to buy, and so on. Regardless of our status in this world, making choices is the great equalizer. But, how often do we think about the potential impact of those choices?

Each time we make a choice, we give up the opportunity to do something else. Going to college means we give up the chance to work during the hours we're in class, and we may end up sacrificing time away from family and friends to work evenings and weekends. No one can have it all, even though it seems like those superstars have found a way to do so. Many of them give up privacy for stardom or face long hours in the studio rehearsing while others are out having fun.

Why would we make such a choice? Because we see that the long-term benefits will pay off. They outweigh the short-term cost of "depriving" ourselves.

Examining our financial futures is much the same. The world we face is growing more complex each day, as are our financial options, and research shows that few of us are prepared to deal with those options. That means when we are required to make a choice about our finances, we often end up guessing. We breathe a sigh of relief if right, but can wreck our future if wrong.

Most of our financial problems do not necessarily stem from a lack of money. Instead, they result from not understanding how to manage the resources available. Those resources include consumer credit, insurance, savings, investments, career opportunities, and, yes, money.

Not-So-Fun Facts

- Studies show that students who work up to 15 hours a week during the school year actually do better academically than students who don't work.
- Finances are the most common reason college students give for dropping out.
- A recent survey by USAA found that more than one-fifth of students plan to spend over $1,000 furnishing their dorm rooms.
- Students often try to buy social acceptance or the notice of the opposite sex.
- Cars, although one of the most desirable extras on campus, are also the biggest budget busters.
- Those who learn too late discover that students who live like professionals while in college are often doomed to live like students when they are professionals.

Source: Kim Clark, "ECON 101: College Is Time to Budget," *U.S. News & World Report*, 12/12/2005, Vol. 139, Issue 22, pp. 62–63.

Money problems are generally associated with a variety of less-than-pleasant outcomes. For example, it is frequently cited as one of the top reasons for divorce. It is a major source of stress, leading to additional problems at home and on the job. It also affects our mental and physical health. While we can debate the old saying that "money is the root of all evil," there is little debate that the financial problems resulting from mismanaging money are the source of many of life's troublesome times.

Can you imagine Carrie Underwood, Kelly Clarkson, or Taylor Hicks just guessing about what songs to sing on *American Idol?* Of course not—so why would we risk our financial futures on simply guessing? While luck may help win a hand of blackjack, it is not a reliable plan for our future.

So, what do you need to do? We need to approach our finances with a plan for success. Being informed about our options and setting goals are good places to start. Knowledge is our best defense against poor choices that rob our time, energy, and bank accounts. And, setting goals keeps us focused on what is important to us.

Today, the average college student graduates owing about $22,000 in debt— just about $5,000 less than the average starting salary. If that $22,000 has an

Livin' Large: Top 10 Tips for Setting Personal Goals

1. **Take a positive approach.** Instead of thinking of how to avoid something, think of how to reach it or succeed. Positive thoughts are always more motivating! Besides, who wants to live life based only on "don't"?

2. **Determine what is important to you.** While others have hopes and dreams for our lives, we will strive harder to reach goals that are ours— not ones prescribed for us. Of course, we want to be considerate of family members and special friends in the process, but that doesn't mean we must sacrifice our future just to please them.

3. **Think of it as a process.** It's okay to set precise dates for accomplishing certain goals, but each one is a step to the next level. Life is much more like assembling a jigsaw puzzle than taking a photo. We start with a picture in mind, then build the edges to provide a good foundation for completing the inside. It's all about putting the small pieces together rather pushing one button!

4. **Be realistic, but don't underestimate your own potential.** We can't all be superstars, but we can be financially independent and have peace of mind.

5. **Prioritize.** Some things are more important than others; only you can determine which is which. Working on those goals at the top of your list will keep you focused and increase your potential of accomplishing them.

6. **Make time for success.** "Rome wasn't created in a day." "Failing to plan is planning to fail." "No pain. No gain." You've heard all those clichés. Each reminds us that success isn't microwave popcorn. We need to think carefully about our life plan and how we want to live it.

7. **Focus on your personal performance.** We all know that life happens, and some things are simply out of our control. However, our response to those situations is not. Regardless of what happens, we maintain total responsibility for how we react and how we conduct our lives. Learning to draw satisfaction from our performance in any storm will take us a long way!

8. **Put goals in writing.** Having goals in writing provides a good reminder of what is important. It will keep us from making choices that divert our attention and our financial resources.

9. **Write goals on paper, not in cement.** About once a year, review your goals to see if you are on track or want to make changes. As we move through different life stages, our goals are likely to change. Remaining flexible and being comfortable with changes helps you take advantage of those opportunities.

10. **Enjoy the ride.**

interest rate of 8 percent and we make the minimum payments, it will take about 30 years to pay off. Starting a career making monthly payments on debt that is equal to our monthly rent requires some significant changes in the way we live. But, eliminating or reducing the deficit allows us to put aside more for our future and accumulate greater wealth.

Most statistics today show a less than glowing financial future for young adults, but it doesn't have to be that way. Remember, our future is our choice. And the choices we make today can have a dramatic impact on our future. No one wants to be 30 years old and still paying off the laptop purchased in the first year of college. Taking charge of our finances ensures we have a future that rocks!

For more on setting goals, complete Backstage Pass on page 77.

CHAPTER TWO

JOB HUNTING AND CAREERS

Each of us can name friends or family members who are successful without a college education. The same is true of several wealthy, big-name entertainers. A number of them opted to pass on college and head straight to the recording studio. But, we can't all sing like Luciano Pavarotti, Barry White, Shania Twain, or Mariah Carey. If so, there would be no reason to go to their concerts or buy their CDs. Their talent would not be unique and their earnings would be greatly reduced. Most of us, however, need an edge; we need something to help develop our abilities and distinguish us from the crowd. A college education is one way to do that.

One of the most important aspects of a college education is that it prepares us for careers, which are different from simply "jobs". A job is a place where we go to work on a regular basis, draw a paycheck, and go home. A career means we strategically and purposefully seek a place of employment and a position that will allow us to grow and develop professionally. It also means we need to continually upgrade our skill sets by participating in professional development opportunities and professional organizations. There is nothing wrong with pursuing a job, but we can get the vocational training we need faster and cheaper at a trade school than on a college campus. However, for a professional career we need a college experience that rounds out our educational experience by expanding our thinking and knowledge base.

A 2004 report released by the U.S. Census Bureau noted the following average annual incomes for workers 18 and older:

No High School Diploma	$18,734
High School Diploma	$27,915
Bachelor's Degree	$51,206
Advanced College Degree	$74,602
Professional Degrees (JD, MD, DVM or DDS)	$99,300

Source: *Educational Attainment in the United States*, U.S. Census Bureau, 2004.

So, just in case you're wondering why you enrolled in college or if it is really worth it to stay in school, these figures should substantiate that decision. Over a lifetime, a college graduate will earn an average of $1 million more than someone with a high school diploma.

For women, the gains are especially impressive. According to recent data from the U.S. Bureau of Labor Statistics, women who graduated from college were earning about 76 percent more than women with a high school diploma in 2004. In 1979, that difference was only 43 percent.

As more educated, younger workers enter the labor force and replace older, less educated workers, these numbers should continue improving. And, that places greater importance on a college degree, along with the need for pursuing advanced degrees or certifications.

Of course, having a college degree does not guarantee the average income nor does it grant automatic success in life or a career. What it does is prepare us for pursuing our financial goals and professional dreams. People attend college for a variety of reasons and not all of them relate to getting a job. For some, it is a quest for personal fulfillment or self-improvement; for others, it is simply to pursue knowledge. Regardless of the reason we attend, we are doing so in record numbers. More than 1 million students earned a college degree in 2000, and about 29 percent of persons in the United States aged 25 to 34 have a college degree today, an increase from 23 percent in 1992.

Pursuing a college degree is expensive and it consumes a lot of our time, but it also pays benefits beyond the annual salary. Some of these benefits include:

- opening doors to more career opportunities
- increasing personal social skills
- offering greater potential for promotions
- increasing the dollar value and number of fringe benefits

- increasing lifetime earnings and savings
- reducing potential for long-term unemployment
- enjoying healthier lives
- being less dependent on social welfare programs
- increasing professional mobility
- reducing propensity for criminal acts and incarceration
- improving quality of life for offspring
- increasing participation in civic and volunteer activities, including charitable giving
- improving overall decision-making abilities

Education pays off for individuals as well as for society in general. And, interestingly, it pays off for students from all walks of life (regardless of race, ethnicity, gender, or socioeconomic background)—even though it does not necessarily benefit everyone equally. For example, men with professional degrees will actually earn about $2 million more than their female counterparts over their work lives. Also, college educated Hispanic and African-American workers tend to earn slightly less than women over their lifetime, but these gaps are closing as society changes.

Women, however, are still not fairing as well. According to General Accounting Office (GAO) *Report GAO-04-35,* full-time working women earned about 80 cents for every dollar earned by men in 2001. Even when including factors such as occupation, industry, race, marital status, and job tenure, the gap remains and is relatively unchanged since the early 1980s. The study concludes that the chief reason for this disparity is the differences in men's and women's work patterns, including more leave from work to care for family.

Did You Know . . .

When you submit a resume to a potential employer, you may have only about 30 to 60 seconds to grab their attention. This means you need to do something to set yourself apart from the rest of the stack. Have you ever filled out a slip for a drawing and folded your entry a certain way before putting it in the box with everyone else's piece of paper? Well, you were trying to improve your odds by making your entry easier to select. Resumes and job applications are somewhat similar. While folding them or printing them on neon yellow paper are not recommended, you can take steps to distinguish yourself with a well-organized, concise, and targeted resume.

GETTING A JOB

Even with a college degree in hand, finding employment is challenging. Many years ago, people would send out hundreds of resumes hoping someone would invite them for an interview. Today, some people take a similar route by posting their resume on various websites hoping a potential employer will find a match. (We need to be very careful about what we post online because we don't know who will be reading it, in attempt to steal information about us.)

Also keep in mind that personal contacts through family, friends, professors, and internships are often better sources of employment than relying solely on Internet postings and web sites.

Tips for Job Interviews

- Prepare a detailed resume to take with you in case a prospective employer wants more information.
- Select a list of your most relevant achievements to discuss during the interview.
- Be truthful! Nothing will catch up with you faster than a little white lie.
- Be prepared to give the interviewer a 30-second "advertisement" about yourself and your career goals. Include at least one piece of personal information to give them a better idea of who you are as a person.
- Dress professionally for the job you aspire to get. Even if you are interviewing for an entry-level position, dress professionally to show respect for yourself and the company.
- Relax and be yourself. Avoid role-playing or faking it. Seasoned interviewers will see through you immediately and send you packing!
- Practice asking and answering questions with friends or family members, and rehearse your delivery in front of a mirror, watching for any annoying behaviors.
- Smile. Believe it or not, employers want happy employees! They also want employees who are interested in their jobs and are pleasant to work with.
- Maintain eye contact during the interview. No one wants to look at the top of your head while they are talking with you.
- Get business cards from the people you meet and follow up with a thank you note or email. Good manners and a personal touch are in your favor.

For most of us, the job search begins with a resume. A resume is a brief summary of our educational experiences, our skills, our work experiences, and our accomplishments. Many human resource experts suggest including a career goal or objective statement at the beginning of the resume to grab a reader's attention, like a headline in the newspaper or a teaser commercial for an upcoming television program. If our career statement announces our top talents, experiences, accomplishments, and qualities, it encourages them to read more about us— especially if we target our statement to match the employer's needs for this specific position. At the same time, every tidbit of information in our resume must be honest and accurate. Why risk a career on one lie or fabrication of facts? It is a huge risk to take, and not worth it.

Writing a high-impact resume takes time and effort because one size does not fit all people or situations. In today's competitive job market, a well-written resume may be the one distinguishing reason we are invited to come for an interview. Taking the time to research resume writing tips and templates increases our odds of finding the best way to present ourselves to a potential employer—and starts the process for landing the job of our dreams.

One of the trends today is referring potential employers to a personal website. We must be very careful about what is posted on that site before asking an employer to view it. While pictures of partying, clowning, and relaxed clothing are funny to friends, they probably will not impress someone who wants us to represent their company. Postings on that personal website are reflections of our character, our values, our level of maturity, and our ability to handle

Tips for Job Interview Appearance

- Dress conservatively. Even if you aren't, the corporate environment generally is. So, avoid bright, flowery clothing with flashy patterns and gemstones. Solid dark colors, such a navy blue, black, or dark gray, are recommended. But, put away your "casual Friday" attire if you want to nail that interview!

- Ask about the dress code. You may want to ask someone in human resources about the dress code before the interview. Some companies require female employees to wear skirts and pantyhose. If that is the case, women would not want to walk into the interview wearing slacks. It's a similar situation for men and ties. It's perfectly acceptable (and encouraged) to ask about the dress code before the interview.

- Dress comfortably. If you are not accustomed to wearing suits, nylons, heels, ties, or other professional attire, start wearing it occasionally to become more comfortable with the style. Appearing to play dress up can be distracting for both you and the interviewer.

- Be clean and clean cut—you personally as well as your clothing. Avoid an abundance of accessories, jewelry, facial hair, cologne, or perfume. Empty all the junk (big key rings, lighters, etc.) from your pockets, and avoid wearing clothing that is stained or wrinkled. Also, leave the dangling earrings, facial jewelry, and dog collars at home!

- Show good hygiene. Yes, take a shower and be sure that your hands and nails are clean, your hair is combed, your face is washed, and your teeth are brushed. It may sound silly to mention, but it's so important!

- And, finally, leave the chewing gum at home! Nothing is worse than trying to talk with someone smacking away on a piece of gum. Carry mints if you need something to keep your breath fresh and your mouth moist.

responsibilities. Offensive language and unflattering photos send warning signs to most employers, giving them an easy excuse to toss our application. So, we need to be careful how we portray ourselves on personal websites or even sites such as myspace.com or facebook.com.

If our resume is successful, we will be asked to go interview for that job. While a resume is a chance to impress a potential employer on paper, a job interview is the opportunity for us to "wow" them in person. Interviewing for a job requires almost as much preparation as the resume. When called for the interview, it is appropriate to ask with whom we will be interviewing. Will it be someone in the human resources office, the potential supervisor, or someone else? Some interviews may involve more than one person, a meeting with potential colleagues, lunch with key staff members, a presentation of some kind, or a written test. So, it is perfectly acceptable to ask about the process in order to be properly prepared. Having sufficient upfront information will reduce our anxiety level, allowing us to relax and be ourselves.

Dressing for a job interview is also important. Unless we are interviewing to go on the road with a rock band or to join the circus, we want to present a professional image. After all, packaging is important to the sale of a product—and it is our only opportunity to show off the quality of our product (ourselves!). While most of us are accustomed to casual styles, a job interview is not the time to show our latest fashions or basic college attire.

CONGRATULATIONS! YOU'RE HIRED!

Isn't that the news we want to hear? But, hey, wait a minute. Are they talking about sending you to school or to training? If they do, that's the sign that employers care about their companies and their employees. It's an additional benefit, like health insurance or retirement plans. Such benefits are valuable additions to your salary.

Most of us seem to think that once we land a job, learning and education stop. But, reality is just the opposite. Continuing to improve our human capital with certifications, on-the-job training, workshops, seminars, and the like is critically important for our careers.

The best gift we give ourselves is learning how to learn. It becomes the difference in staying at an entry-level position or advancing to the CEO's office. So, we should take advantage of each opportunity to improve our skill sets. Now is the time to prepare for that life-long learning experience by developing good study habits and appreciating the complete value of a broad-based college education.

FROM "HEAD OF THE CLASS" TO "HEAD OF THE ORGANIZATION"— LIVIN' LARGE PROFESSIONALLY

1. Start learning how to learn, and continue practicing that mantra throughout your career.

2. Build an appropriate resume to open the first door for you. Resumes do not need to be long, but they do need to be complete and accurate to truthfully reflect who you are and how you can benefit the organization.

3. Take the opportunity to hone your interview skills. Practice job interviews with a faculty member, a friend, a colleague at work, or a mentor. If you have a part-time job, you might even ask your employer to give you a mock interview for your current job. The more you practice, the more you will develop those skills.

4. Make the job hunt a job in itself. If you take a professional attitude of working hard and following every possible lead, you will have an advantage over those who view job hunting as a hobby. Getting the job of your dreams doesn't just happen. It requires time, energy, and patience.

5. What you know is still important. While having friends in the right places can help, you still have to sell yourself on every interview and every day on the job thereafter. Those friends might help get you in the door, but only you can determine what happens once inside.

6. Send a thank-you note to everyone you met during the job interview. Few people today take the time to say "thanks"—especially in writing. Purchase a supply of professional-looking thank-you notes and make a habit of writing a brief note mentioning something the two of you discussed during the interview. It shows you listen, plus it shows you have class!

7. Be careful about getting "too familiar" with the interviewers. Unless specifically asked, it is always appropriate to address men as *Mr.* and women as *Ms.* (pronounced *Mzz*). Even though you call your parents' friends by their first names, it is not proper to refer to interviewers in this manner.

8. Shake hands and make eye contact with your interviewers. A good, strong clutch in a handshake says something about your personality. So, forget about limp, wimpy handshakes if you want to succeed in getting that job.

9. Research the newspapers, corporate annual reports, magazines, and other materials to find information on the company before the interview. Showing that you know about the company—its current products, trends, reputation in the community, and other important aspects—tells the interviewer that you are serious about joining the company.

10. Enjoy the hunt. Becoming comfortable with who you are, how you dress, and what you want from an employer will go a long way in showing you are prepared and ready to work for them. You will feel much more relaxed during interviews and more confident in your own abilities.

For more on interviewing, complete Backstage Pass on page 79.

CHAPTER THREE

BUDGETING: BUILDING A ROAD MAP

Talk about a reality check! Trying to pay bills each month without knowing where the money will come from is often a daily reality. Yet, the thought of budgeting sounds so overwhelming for most people. While we've all heard those songs about living on love, it's difficult to find a merchant who will accept it as payment for purchases or a bill collector who appreciates its value.

Many people today live with "more month at the end of the money," instead of the other way around. It's difficult to reach our financial goals when we have no plan to get there. A budget is very simply that: a tool for tracking how much we make and how much we spend. Having a budget in place allows us to make informed choices about our money.

The amount of money we earn is not nearly as important as the amount we spend. Wealthy people can face financial ruin just as quickly as people who live on limited incomes. Overspending or reckless financial behavior is the greatest impediment to reaching personal goals or dreams for our families.

Budgets allow us to be in control of our finances, to be proactive with our spending decisions instead of reactive to our emotions. Think of it like a road map. If we're only out for a Sunday drive, then it doesn't matter where we go. But, if we have a specific destination in mind, we get out the map to help take the best route. That's what a budget does for our goals. It creates a road map to our dreams by guiding our financial decisions. In addition, a budget builds a safety net that helps prevent financial disasters from wrecking our future.

Budgets are not necessarily a "diet" that eliminates or cuts spending; instead, budgets promote smart spending. Setting up and following a budget keeps us focused on what is important, reduces impulse buying, and reduces the potential of bankruptcy or overextending our capacity to manage debt. Spending smart is much easier than increasing our income to cover those bills!

If the word "budget" sounds too overwhelming or restrictive, call it a "spending plan" or a "debt busting plan."

BUT, WHERE DO WE START?

First, we need to be realistic about our spending habits. Do we really know how much money we spend each month, and do we really know where that money goes? Having a spending plan will help us answer those questions. It will also help prevent us from overspending by impulse buying or making purchases that don't fit our financial goals.

A good place to start is by writing down everything we buy for one month. That includes EVERYTHING. Most of us will be shocked at the results. It's hard to believe that one gourmet coffee purchased every morning adds up to some $60 a month, or $720 a year! And, "supersizing" those trips to the fast-food restaurants once a day basically doubles the amount spent. Most of us could add an extra $1,500 each year with very little change in our actions.

Tracking spending can be done two different ways: one, carry a small notepad in your pocket and write down each purchase when you make it; two, get a receipt for every purchase and write them all down when you get home each evening. With the second option, it's best to carry something to jot down any transactions for which receipts are not available. For example, if you give five dollars to a friend, it's probably easier to write it down than to ask her for a receipt!

Once we have those expenses recorded, we can put them into various categories such as rent or housing payments, entertainment, education, clothing, food, eating out, insurance, utilities, hobbies, and the like. By taking this action, the budget mirrors our actual spending habits instead of a generic form that may or may not be appropriate for our behaviors. Totaling the expenditures for each category shows the actual dollar amount we spend each month.

The next step is to see how our spending compares with our income. When you total all of those expenditures, is there enough coming in each month to continue that level of spending? Or, are you using credit cards to artificially increase your monthly allotment? Did you remember to include those credit card payments in your monthly expenses?

If we continue spending more each month than we make, we're headed for financial disaster because we are robbing ourselves of any future income. It may seem like fun to accumulate those purchases, but it's no fun to face years of paying for them. Those payments last much longer than most products! So, now is the time to reduce the amount spent in order to match income with expenses.

But wait. Did you remember to include a payment to yourself? Setting aside some amount each month—no matter how small—for an emergency savings account is one of the smartest steps to take in building a budget. After all, who is more important than you or your family?

Another area frequently overlooked is tithing or making charitable donations. Giving to others is almost as important as paying yourself. As a general rule, financial planners tend to advocate the idea of contributing as much as we can comfortably afford to give without putting additional financial strains on our budget. In some cases, we may choose to supplement that dollar amount with our personal time and talents to the organization to make up for any shortfalls in our financial gifts. Regardless of the amount, we want to set a habit of meeting our responsibility to religious or charitable organizations.

If we are already accumulating debt that needs immediate attention, most experts recommend setting up a separate category in our budgets called "debt reduction" to pay down that debt as soon as possible. While we must be realistic about how much we can allocate to repaying debts, no one can question the validity of making it a priority. After all, the faster we pay them off, the more money we'll have to save for future purchases, making us less reliant on credit.

Any budget or spending plan must reflect our own individual lifestyles. Otherwise, it is impossible to stay with it. If the plan involves more than one person, then it is important to reach some consensus about common goals and a shared commitment to achieving them. This process may require negotiation and compromise, but will reduce the potential for future conflicts. Money problems are one of the leading causes of divorce or marital tensions. Having an open and honest discussion about money may not prevent such problems, but it will certainly provide a means for understanding the source of those problems and offer opportunities for resolving them.

Being realistic about our financial habits and financial needs is also important when establishing our spending plan. For example, eliminating all fun from our budget is a sure sign it will fail. However, spending 50 percent of our budget on entertainment is equally unrealistic. Finding a balance between what we need and what we want will help ensure we stick with our plan and accomplish our goals.

To get an accurate accounting of our income, we need to include all sources received on a regular basis and allocate it equally each month. If we receive some kind of annual allotment from a trust fund, student loans, or other sources, then that amount would be divided by 12 and added to our monthly earnings.

So what happens if we've added up the expenses and made a few changes, but still have less income than we need each month?

Most of us would automatically cut out the money we pay ourselves and reduce the amount we included in debt reduction. But, those may not be the best choices. What happens if the car breaks down? If we haven't set aside something for those emergencies and we have no spare change, then most of us turn to credit cards. So, here we go—committing more future income to pay for today's spending. Continuing that habit makes it impossible to break even, let alone get ahead. Who wants to be paying for those car repairs 10 years after it was traded in for a newer model?

For an eye-opening illustration, try the American Express *Saving or Spending Big Calculator*. Enter the cost and frequency of a habit or indulgence and how many years you expect it to continue. Click a button and see not only how much you'll spend over the specified time period, but how much that same amount would grow to if you invested it at various rates of return. (Source: Budgeting by Deborah Fowler at *http://www.financialplan.about .com.*)

Looking for an online budget calculator? The U.S. Department of Education has one on its Federal Student Aid website. This particular budget calculator is designed specifically for college students and lists some of their most important expenses and resources, such as tuition, books, scholarships, etc. For more information, go to *http://www.ed.gov/offices/ OSFAP/DirectLoan/Budget- Calc/budget.html.* A similar calculator for college students can be found at *http://www.accessgroup.org/c alculators/in_schlbud.htm.* Check both sites out for help in preparing your personal spending plan.

Instead, we can look for other ways to trim spending or increase income. For most of us, it may mean we have to reduce our housing or transportation costs or reduce the number of times we drive through the fast-food window each week. Making a few tough choices today, however, will reap rewards for tomorrow. Wouldn't it be better to live in a smaller apartment now and have the money to make the down payment on a dream home in a few years? And, wouldn't it be better to drive a less expensive, more economical vehicle right now and be able to pay bills than to drive the hottest car available to the bankruptcy attorney's office? Sound extreme? It may not be so far out. Young adults between the ages of 18 and 24 are the fastest growing segment of the population filing bankruptcy today, primarily from taking on more debt than they can repay.

Oftentimes, our spending includes purchases that really aren't necessary or that don't contribute to our overall quality of life. We just buy them because they're there. Too many of us seem to use shopping as a recreational activity instead of choosing a less expensive option, such as walk in the park or at the local track. When budgets are extremely tight, we can buy fewer frivolous items (magazines, CDs, etc.), use coupons on those products we purchase regularly, or shop at discount stores for the best prices to add a few dollars each month to our savings or debt reduction accounts. If we can identify which purchases are our personal budget busters, we can avoid situations that trigger the buying response and help us meet our monthly targets.

Another option is taking on a part-time job to offset those additional costs. Depending on our situations, this option can present additional problems— especially for those already working, going to school, and managing other responsibilities. Having no time for school, no time for self, and no time for friends or family gets old quickly, so it's usually a good short-term solution rather than a long-term answer to the predicament.

Developing the discipline to "live within our means" is one of the greatest gifts we can give ourselves. It frees us from the stress and pressure of bills and bill collectors, and it increases our future earnings for the things we really enjoy. Budgets, spending plans, or whatever we choose to call them provide a framework for financial freedom—the freedom to achieve our goals, our dreams, and the lifestyle we want for our family.

Whether country, rock, or disco, plenty of songs have been written about the life of the working class. Many of them depict a rather bleak picture of living paycheck-to-paycheck while others make reference to their dreams. Most of us identify with those words. We work hard for our money—having a budget will help us keep some of it for ourselves and our families instead of giving it all away to others.

LIVIN' LARGE BY SPENDING LESS

1. Make a list when you go shopping and buy only what's on your list.
2. Avoid malls or online shopping when you are sad, bored, or depressed; it increases the temptation to spend.
3. Forget about the Joneses. You don't have to keep up with anybody. Besides, they may be swimming in debt. Owing a million dollars doesn't make you a millionaire!
4. Plan ahead. Birthdays come at the same time every year and so do the major holidays. Make those gifts part of your "planned spending" by setting aside a small amount each month.
5. The cost of the gift does not equal how much you care for the recipient, so spend less than you originally planned. If friends don't understand "it's the thought that counts," maybe you need new friends!
6. Pay bills on time. Those late fees are very expensive!
7. Use credit for major purchases or emergencies. And, that late night run for pizza is NOT an emergency!
8. Avoid buying food at convenience stores. While more convenient, they are also more expensive.
9. Be a bargain hunter. Compare prices before making a final decision about your purchases.
10. Find fun ways to spend your time, not your money.

For more on tracking your expenses, and spending plans and budgets, complete Backstage Pass on pages 81 and 82.

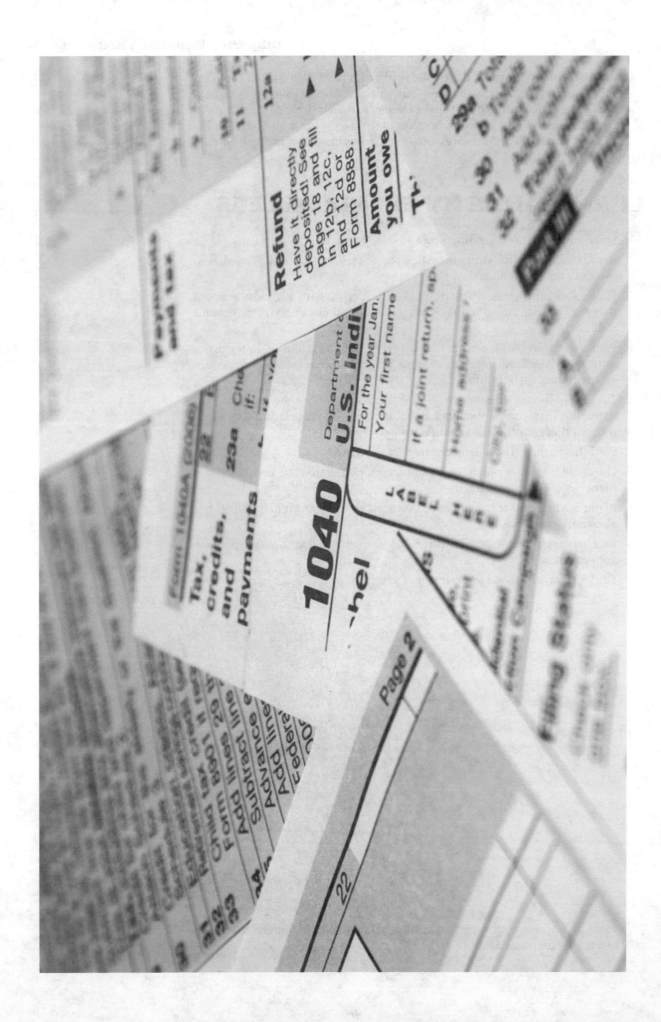

CHAPTER FOUR
TAXES

Many of our favorite singing sensations hold concerts in somewhere around 200 different locations each year. Life "on the road" is frequently documented by several big-name entertainers. Living on a bus and traveling to a different location every day may seem like fantasy, but it is the only life for many of today's biggest stars.

What many of us don't realize is that entertainers in those road shows are required to file a state income tax return in each state where they perform. In addition, many of the cities where they perform can levy personal income taxes on anyone earning income within their city limits. Just think about it—having to pay income tax in some 30 states and 50 cities. It certainly doesn't sound like fun, even for those earning as much as they do.

Fortunately, most of us will never have to worry about completing so many tax returns each year. But that doesn't mean we can't use some help when it comes to dealing with our personal tax responsibilities.

Developing an effective tax strategy will get us further down the road in meeting our financial goals by minimizing our tax liability each year. And who doesn't like to legally save money on their taxes? It's okay for government to get its fair share, but there's no reason to pay more than we must.

Most of us pay personal income taxes on our adjusted gross income—not on every dollar we earn. Our adjusted gross income is simply the income we receive from all sources minus any adjustments, such as payments to our retirement plan. Our taxable income is what we have left over after taking all deductions and exemptions. Most taxpayers are eligible to take a standard deduction each year, reducing our tax liability. However, we may also have the opportunity to itemize our deductions, allowing us to subtract an even larger amount. Itemized deductions include expenses for health care, state and local taxes, personal property taxes, interest paid on a home mortgage, gifts to charity and other not-for-profit organizations, job-related expenses, tax preparation fees, and investment-related expenses.

One key tax-planning strategy is to track our expenses throughout the year using a spreadsheet or personal finance program. Such a spreadsheet can help us quickly compare our itemized expenses with our standard deduction. If the dollar amount of the total itemized deductions is greater than the standard deduction, then obviously we should itemize because it will reduce our income tax by the greatest amount. We do need to keep in mind, however, that the standard deduction depends on on our filing status and is not just one standard amount.

Did You Know . . .

If you are self-employed, then you have to pay both the employer and employee portions of social security and Medicare. That will eat 15.3 percent of your net earnings. And, if you don't make estimated tax payments to the federal and state government every quarter, you could face some hefty penalties.

Basically, we have three different options to reduce our tax payments: increase our deductions, decrease our income, and use any eligible tax credits.

INCREASING DEDUCTIONS

Home mortgage payments and charitable donations are two of the largest deductions most individuals will have. While increasing our mortgage payments can be difficult, we certainly can look for ways to increase our charitable contributions—which includes giving used clothing or household items to various not-for-profit organizations such as religious and social organizations. One of the most important aspects of increasing our deductions is keeping detailed records of our spending and donations.

Several software packages are currently available at reasonable prices to help track our spending, donations, and deductible items. Or, we can seek professional advice from a tax accountant to help set up our records. Possible tax deductions

Did You Know . . .

Some people seem to think that getting a large tax refund in April is one of their greatest accomplishments. But, is it really so great? If the federal government owes you money, it means you have been overpaying them every month of the year and they have been using your money—without paying you for it.

It also means that you have invested in the government at zero rate of return—when you could have been earning interest on YOUR money. Why give the government a free loan?

Ideally, you want to break even when you file your income tax return each year or owe a very small amount. It is certainly smarter planning to use the government's money instead of vice versa.

range from personal expenditures on health care to job-related items and investment costs. But, without good records to support our spending behavior, we will have a difficult time accounting for our deductions.

DECREASING INCOME

While decreasing our income just to save a few dollars in taxes sounds a bit far-fetched, we should remember that our goal is to reduce our adjusted gross income (our taxable income)—not our gross income. One of the best ways to accomplish a drop in our adjustable gross income is to increase our contributions to our 401(k) or another similar retirement plan offered at work. Another option is opening an Individual Retirement Account (IRA). Think of it this way: We can reduce our taxes by paying ourselves!

IS EITC 4U?

Looking to reduce your tax liability? Then check out the Earned Income Tax Credit (EITC). EITC can reduce or even eliminate any taxes owed.

USING ELIGIBLE TAX CREDITS

Tax credits are a dollar-for-dollar reduction of our tax liabilities. Some examples are child-care expenses, elderly or disabled credits, adoption expenses, some retirement savings, and some education expenses. Not all tax credits are the same. In fact, some credits are refundable, meaning that taxes could be reduced to the point where we receive a refund instead of having to pay any taxes. Because of the great variance in using tax credits, we need to carefully research our options or get professional advice.

TAXES FOR STUDENTS

Being a student does not automatically exempt us from paying taxes. The following kinds of income often received by students are generally taxable:

- Pay for services performed
- Self-employment income
- Investment income
- Certain scholarships and fellowships

When figuring how much income to report, we should include everything received in payment for our services, such as wages, salaries, and tips. Wages and salary are fairly easy to track because our employers will report them on our statements and we will receive W-2 tax forms, "Wage and Tax Statements," with our year-end totals. The amounts on the W-2 are the numbers we use when preparing our income tax return.

Tips, on the other hand, require the most substantiation on our part. All tips we receive are income and should be reported as part of our taxable income. It is in our best interest to keep a daily record of tips. (Note: The Internal Revenue Service (IRS) even provides **Form 4070A,** "Employee's Daily Record of Tips," to help). If the amount of tips received is $20 or more in any one calendar month while working for one employer, we must report the total amount to the IRS by the 10th day of the next month. Our report should include the following information:

- Name, address, and social security number
- Employer's name, address, and business name (if it is different from the employer's name)
- The month (or the dates of any shorter period) in which the tips were received
- The total tips reported for that period of time

Our employer will use this information to compute our social security, Medicare, and other withholdings.

In addition to paying taxes on our wages, salary, and tips, we also must report any income from our investments, such as interest paid to us on checking and savings accounts. We may also have to pay taxes on scholarships, fellowships, and other similar awards unless all amounts go to pay for tuition, books, and other supplies for our coursework. Any questions about what is taxable should be directed to the person or organization providing the funds or an accountant specializing in taxes.

Example 1

Tammy Graves receives a $6,000 fellowship grant that is not designated for any specific use. Tammy is a degree candidate. She spends $5,500 for tuition and $500 for her personal expenses. Tammy is required to include $500 in income.

Your Tax Refund

Did you get a tax refund this year? What are your plans—a new car, new iPod, a summer vacation, or to just go to the mall and see what you come with? How about choosing one of the following ideas? No, this list isn't as exciting as spending money—but it shows how you can make money rock!

- Pay extra on credit card bills. Paying down your debt is the best gift you can give yourself and your family! Depending upon the amount of the refund and your credit card balances, you may even be able to pay off one of them—then you can add the amount paid on that bill to either your savings or to another monthly credit card payment.
- Add to your emergency fund. If you don't have one, use it as "seed" money to start growing your emergency account. Having an emergency fund will keep you from going into debt when surprise expenses come along.
- Start a college fund or savings account for your children. Many states have a college fund that is easy to set up so you can save for your children to attend college. And in many states, you will get a deduction on next year's taxes.
- Open a Roth IRA. You've already paid taxes on the refund you are receiving, so you can open a Roth IRA with no additional tax liability.

Example 2

Ursula Harris, a degree candidate, receives a $2,000 scholarship, with $1,000 specifically designated for tuition and $1,000 specifically designated for living expenses. Her tuition is $1,600. She may exclude $1,000 from income, but the other $1,000 designated for living expenses is taxable and must be included in income.

(Source of examples: Internal Revenue Service Publication "Taxable Income for Students" available at *http://www.irs.gov/individuals/students/article/0,,id=96674,00.html*.)

Most estimates are that we work somewhere around 80 days out of the year for the federal government to pay all of our taxes—plus additional days to pay our state taxes. So, earning money that we can use to pay our bills, save for our futures, or purchase goods and services doesn't start until sometime in May. In a market-based economy like that of the United States, it is part of our responsibility as citizens to pay our taxes. However, it is also our responsibility to provide for our families and for our future. Understanding our rights as taxpayers will help us meet those responsibilities, today and tomorrow.

IRS Withholding Calculator

The Internal Revenue Service provides an online calculator that will help you determine if you are having too much or too little income tax withheld from your paycheck. It is not a replacement for Form W-4, but you might find it easier to use than the worksheets that accompany Form W-4. You may use the results of this program to help you complete a new Form W-4, which you will submit to your employer. The calculator is available at *http://www.irs.gov/individuals/article/0,,id=96196,00.html*.

For more on taxes, complete Backstage Pass on pages 83–86.

CREDIT CARDS AND CASH MANAGEMENT

CHAPTER FIVE

PAPER OR PLASTIC?

How many times do we hear that question when bagging our groceries? It's not only a good question when sacking purchases, but it's also a good question to consider when paying for them.

Few things are as easy as whipping out a credit card and charging goods or services. Buying something we really want gives us pleasure and credit cards help fuel that feeling of instant gratification—until the bill arrives at the end of the month. Then, the pleasure is gone. Paying bills isn't fun and the goods we got some pleasure out of during the first of the month are limiting our spending power at the end of the month—and for many months to follow! Like a light switch, immediate gratification can turn on us quickly, temporarily or permanently disrupting our financial future.

Credit cards are generally used to bridge the gap between what we want and what we can afford to buy, especially when living on a limited budget. And, hey, it looks impressive to pull out a gold or platinum card to buy lunch at a restaurant. But, do you realize paying with credit is similar to taking out a bank loan to buy that burger or pizza? And, by placing no constraints on buying on credit, we can lead ourselves into financial trouble that is hard to escape.

It's hard to believe how accessible credit is these days. If gaining credit card offers were an Olympic sport, we'd all be on the medal stand. Most of us are bombarded daily with preapproved offers, transfer balance offers, checks that just need a signature to be activated, and the like.

Some people are even calling for Congress to pass legislation reducing the aggressive marketing tactics used by many credit card companies, especially the strategies used with high school and college students. Such legislation would not be necessary if we would learn how to "Just Say NO!" Just because they mail us an offer doesn't mean we have to accept. (And by the way, be careful about just tossing all those offers in the trash. Someone may use them to steal your identity and ruin your credit ratings! Be sure to shred all offers before tossing.)

Good credit is invaluable; bad credit is tragic. While credit can be a great financial tool, it can also be easily abused and take us so deep into debt that it takes years to recover. And overspending on credit cards is a certain financial death wish.

Did You Know . . .

The average family has about $8,000 in credit card debt, and about $1,000 of their annual income goes to pay the interest on that debt every year. In fact, over 90 percent of the money a family spends goes toward paying past debt. Credit card debt in the United States grew at an annual rate of 9.2 percent between 1993 and 2003, compared with a 5.2 percent annual increase in personal income.

(Source: Consumer Federation of America, 2000.)

Using credit makes spending very impersonal. It allows us to buy and buy, without stopping to physically count the total amount of those expenditures. Only when we max out a credit card do we think about it being finite—and then most companies will simply increase our credit limit or just charge us for exceeding it. Basically, buying on credit is like having an endless supply of money to fund an endless flow of spending. Buying with cash is different. When the money is gone, the spending stops. Seeing the total amount of cash in our hands helps us better manage our spending habits because we know exactly what we have—and when it will be gone. Coins and currency are tangible; they are real—made from paper and metals. Credit cards are plastic and they represent pretend money; we pretend to have more money than we do.

Living with debt is not pleasant. It simple terms, we are using today's money to pay for yesterday's purchases. And, if that habit continues, we will always have trouble making ends meet. Financial goals become financial myths because it is virtually impossible to save when we are swimming in debt.

Any pleasure received from the purchase is offset by the increased stress of paying the bills. But it doesn't take much imagination to realize that stress from indebtedness takes away from our quality of life, often leaving us with strained relationships with family and friends, depression, or even thoughts of suicide.

If money rocks, then credit rolls. And for most of us, the balance on our credit cards rolls over from one month to another—compounding the interest and increasing the total amount we owe even when we're working to make the payments. The key is learning to manage debt, not having debt manage you.

CURRENT STATISTICS

In 1998, a study by the Education Resources Institute found that almost two-thirds of all college students have at least one credit card, while 20 percent of them have four or more credit cards (Education Resources Institute, June 1998).

In 2000, a study by Nellie Mae reported an increase in those numbers. Their survey found that 78 percent of undergraduates (aged 18–25) and 95 percent of graduate students had at least one card. Undergraduates carried an average balance of $2,748 while graduate students carried an average balance of $4,776. Nellie Mae also found that of the 78 percent of undergraduates with a card; 32% had four or more cards; 13% had credit card debt between $3,000 and $7,000; and 9 percent had credit card debt greater than $7,000 (Nellie Mae, 2000).

Students with high credit card debt face greater problems than just repaying the debt. Recent studies show that increased credit card debt requires students to work more hours to pay down their debt. Taking on the additional responsibility often leads to poor academic performance—and in some cases, it actually requires students to drop out of college or take a reduced load, postponing their graduation dates in order to repay their credit card debt.

But that's not all. Taking few hours and an extra year or two to graduate may also increase the cost of going to college!

Adding more problems, students with high credit card debt have a much harder time repaying student loans once they do graduate.

Furthermore, some employers and graduate schools will actually reject applications from students who had bad credit while in college. And, poor credit ratings make it difficult to lease an apartment, buy a car, or purchase a home once students enter the workforce.

So, before you charge that late-night pizza or download the latest hit, think about the potential long-term consequences of your choice!

LIVIN' LARGE: MANAGING CREDIT

1. Pay your bills on time. Missing a payment will result in additional fees plus higher interest rates, which quickly compound and create more problems.

2. Credit cards are not all bad. They are convenient and safer to carry than cash, and they are a great tool for establishing a good history needed for future credit needs. Credit cards are not a substitute for income. Having good intentions to pay off credit cards is not the same as really paying them off! So, think twice before saying "CHARGE!"

3. Practice discipline when using credit, especially credit cards. They have a purpose and should be used only when absolutely necessary or if you have the money in bank to pay them off each month. A good rule to use is this: Don't buy anything that takes longer to pay off than the product will last.

4. Read your statement and credit terms carefully. That small print is important! And, not all credit cards are the same.

5. Making minimum payments increases the cost of every purchase you make! Just because an item is on sale doesn't mean you have to buy it—especially if you are charging it to your credit card.

6. The only way to get out of debt is to stop spending. No one said it would be fun, but you must stop the bleeding before you can heal.

7. Carrying multiple credit cards is like playing Russian Roulette. There is incredible incentive to use them if they are in your pocket. Find a credit card with a moderate balance and the lowest possible interest rate. If you feel like you need an extra card "just in case," put it on ice. (Put extra cards in a container of water and put the container in your freezer. You can thaw them in case of emergencies. But the time delay gives you time to think—while still giving you the added security of another card.)

8. Keep your credit receipts and balance your card statement just like you balance a checking account. Yes, credit card companies do make mistakes. It also alerts you if someone else is using your card number without your knowledge.

9. If you have charges on multiple credit cards, pay off the one with the highest interest rate first. The easiest way to do this is by paying the minimum on all other credit cards, and paying as much as possible on the high-interest card. Once it is paid off, cut up the card and close your account. Then, add the amount you were paying to the second-highest-interest card and continue until all are paid off. Then, put that amount into your savings account so you won't need to rely on credit for future purchases.

10. If you know you are in credit trouble, get help. There are reliable credit counseling services available in most communities that can provide the assistance you need. If unsure where to go, talk to your banker or a financial advisor. It's probably wise to avoid unscrupulous firms who advertise on TV in the middle of the night.

For more on credit cards, complete Backstage Pass on page 87.

CHAPTER SIX

SCHEMES, SCAMS, AND IDENTITY THEFT

People in the spotlight frequently change their names because they don't like their original name, it's hard to pronounce, or it sounds too much like someone else. For example, Conway Twitty was born Harold Jenkins, Prince (or the artist formerly known as Prince) is actually Prince Rogers Nelson, Ringo Starr was christened Richard Starkey, Jr., and even American icon Bob Hope started life as Leslie Townes Hope. Others, like Sean Combs, have gone through a myriad of name changes—Puffy, Puff Daddy, P. Diddy, Diddy—throughout their career. It is also common to impersonate different stars and make appearances at parties and other entertainment venues. We can only wonder how many Elvises are out there! Sometimes, people will impersonate famous people in hopes of impressing others, just to see what they can get.

Changing a name or using a different name is generally a simple legal process and is perfectly legit—as along as we are still the same person. Impersonating someone can be a little different. It is acceptable when we are doing it only for entertainment purposes, with the clear understanding that we really are not that person. However, we enter dangerous waters when we assume someone else's identity and start passing ourselves off as them.

Unfortunately, famous people are not the only ones who can become victims of identity theft. In fact, identity theft is one of the fastest growing crimes in the United States today. Even though most of us can eventually repair our reputation, reclaiming our identity is a long and costly process—sometimes taking years and costing thousands of dollars.

Identity theft means someone steals our name, reputation, and personal information, using them for their own financial gain. Without ever pointing a gun or seeing our face, they can rob us of our financial assets. Then it is our responsibility to clean up their mess and reestablish our good name and our credit.

The Identity Theft and Assumption Deterrence Act of 1998 made it a federal crime when anyone "knowingly transfers or uses, without lawful authority, a means of identification of another person with the intent to commit, or to aid or abet, any unlawful activity that constitutes a violation of the Federal law, or that constitutes a felony under any applicable State or local law."

Being young or a student does not exempt us from the problem. In fact, being a student may actually make us more vulnerable. Why? Because student information is sometimes readily available and because students tend to take few precautions to protect it. A recent national study found the following:

- Almost half of all college students receive credit card applications on a daily or weekly basis. Many of these students throw out card applications without destroying them.

- Nearly a third of students rarely, if ever, reconcile their credit card and checking account balances.

- Almost 50 percent of students have had grades posted by social security number.

These habits make students good candidates for identity theft.

Monitoring our checking accounts, reconciling our credit card statements each month, and requesting annual copies of our credit reports can help determine if someone is using our name to make purchases for themselves. Once a problem is found, we must take action immediately to minimize our losses. Some of these actions include:

- Close current bank accounts, credit card accounts, and other similar accounts as soon as possible and reopen them with new account numbers. We can request passwords for greater protection, but should be careful about using the usual (mother's maiden name, birth date, social security number, etc.). Most companies today have a fraud unit to help with the process.

- Contact the Social Security Administration, state driver's license bureau, and other groups issuing identification numbers to get replacement numbers and cards. We can also request that they flag our names to ensure no one else can get additional numbers or cards in our name.

- Call the toll-free fraud numbers of the three major consumer credit reporting companies to request a fraud alert on our credit reports. Alerts will help stop the thief from opening new credit accounts or loans in our name.

- Contact law enforcement officials in the city where the theft occurred. If we're not sure where it happened, then we can go to the police department in the city where we live for assistance. If another crime was committed along with it, such as stolen purse or home burglary, then we need to notify the policy immediately.

- File a complaint with the Federal Trade Commission. The FTC maintains a database of identity theft cases used by law enforcement agencies for investigations. Filing a complaint also helps us learn more about identity theft and the problems we can expect.

One of the most complete resources for learning more about identity theft is offered by the Federal Trade Commission at *http://www.consumer.gov/idtheft/ index.html.* It's worth the visit!

SCAMS

In addition to identity theft, we need to beware of possible schemes and scams that take our money and deliver nothing in return. For college students and potential students, scholarship search services and financial aid advice services are one of the most common scams available. Many of these for-profit companies charge high rates for information available free online, in the library, from school counselors, or a variety of other sources. While it is not illegal to charge for "free" information, it is illegal for these companies to take our money and not provide the information. It is also illegal for them to pose as government agencies and make

Did You Know . . .

According to the U.S. Department of Justice, we increase our risk of being a victim if we can answer yes to any of the following questions:

- Do you use your personal computer for online banking transactions?
- Do you use your personal computer to buy merchandise or purchase tickets for travel, concerts, or other services?
- Do you receive credit card offers in the mail? Do you discard these documents before you shred them?
- Do you store personal information in your computer?
- Do you use a cell phone?
- Do you use your social security number for identification?
- Do you have a student loan?

Each of these transactions requires you to share personal information such as your bank and credit card account numbers, your social security number, or your name, address, and phone number. This is the same personal information that identity thieves use to commit fraud.

promises they cannot keep (such as guaranteeing a free ride to our chosen college or university).

Other scams include those designed to get personal information from us via email or the phone, asking us to pay a fee to help transfer money in or out of the country, informing us we have won a contest we never entered, seeking advanced payments for services we did not request, promising to repair our credit, or a multitude of other opportunists wanting to take our money and run. The bottom line is this: Grandma was right when she said "if it's too good to be true, then it probably is!" The problem is, today's con artists are very savvy—so we have to keep up our guard at all times.

Many of today's schemes or scams start with "phishing," a favorite ploy of identity thieves and scammers. When "phishing" for personal information, criminals may work through the Internet by posing as representatives of the IRS, our bank, or other legitimate organizations. Their goal is to trick us into giving them information that can be used to steal money from our accounts or involve us in their scheme. It is a good rule to never disclose personal information in an email, on a website, or over the phone unless we have initiated the contact. If they call, we can hang up. If they email, we can delete it. And if we stumble onto their website, we can close it.

Here is a list of important websites to get additional information on identity theft, schemes, and scams:

- *http://www.consumer.gov/idtheft/index.html* The FTC website is one of the most complete resources for learning more about identity theft and scams.
- *http://www.ftc.gov/ftc/consumer/media _consumeralerts.html* This FTC website offers tips on recognizing and avoiding scams, as well as other valuable consumer information.
- *http://www.sec.gov/investor/pubs/cyberfraud.htm* This site tells how to spot different types of Internet fraud, what the SEC is doing to fight Internet investment scams, and how to use the Internet to invest wisely.
- *http://www.pueblo.gsa.gov/scamsdesc.htm* The Federal Citizen Information Center posts information on current schemes and scams, helping protect us from falling prey to the illegal activities of others.
- *http://www.irs.gov/newsroom/article/ 0,,id=154293,00.html* The IRS issues its list of top tax scams each year.

LIVIN' LARGE: PROTECTING YOURSELF FROM ID THEFT

1. Protect your numbers! That includes numbers on credit cards, bank accounts, savings accounts, social security cards, and personal identification numbers (PINs), to name a few. Keep personal information "personal," and don't give it to anyone unless you initiate the contact. Even then, be sure you are dealing with a reputable company. (Note: The same applies to friends! You cannot be too careful, so make it a rule not to share this kind of information with anyone.)

2. Avoid writing PINs or passwords on ATM or credit cards—and don't carry them with you. For passwords, using a combination of letters and numbers makes it even more difficult for someone to figure out. And remember to change your passwords frequently. Birthdays, addresses, your mother's maiden name, and other similar information are not good passwords because they are too easily discovered.

3. Your social security number (SSN) is your lifeline. With that one number, hackers and thieves can find out almost everything about you. Be very careful about giving your SSN to anyone. While banks, employers, and others may need the information for tax purposes, most people do not have any need for it. Avoid using it on your checks, your driver's license, your resume, or any other ID card.

4. Shred or tear up all personal information before tossing it in the trash can. That includes all credit card receipts, deposit slips, account statements, cancelled checks, unused credit card checks, and other papers containing your personal information—even those unopened credit card offers.

5. Be careful with your mail. Never put bill payments in your home mailbox; take them to the post office or a mail drop. If you're going to be out of town for a couple of days or more, put a hold on your mail until you return. (You can now go online and do this, so it's fast and easy! www.usps.com) If you

believe that any mail is missing from your home mailbox, contact the post office for assistance and notify any potential senders. Credit card bills should come about the same time each month, so watch for them and contact the company immediately if it does not arrive.

6. Review your bank statements, credit card statements, and other accounts monthly to ensure that all charges are correct. If there are any errors or unauthorized charges, contact the issuing institution immediately. Otherwise, you may be held liable for those charges.

7. Order a copy of your credit report once a year from each of the three major credit reporting firms. Review it carefully to be sure that no new accounts or loans have been opened in your name without your permission.

8. When making purchases over the Internet, be sure you are dealing with a recognized, reputable business. It is advisable to have one credit card or one checking card that is used only for online purchases. Even with processes like PayPal, hackers can break through and steal your account numbers. Having one card with a low amount on deposit dedicated to these purchases will limit hackers' access to your personal information and your money.

9. Carry only what you need in your wallet or purse. Just because you have multiple credit cards does not mean you need to carry them with you everywhere you go. Leaving your credit cards at home in a safe, secure place not only protects them from being lost or stolen, it also reduces the temptation to use them. (Never carry your social security card in your wallet.)

10. Remember that the burden of proof is on you! While the other party may be guilty, you have to use your time, your money, and your energy to prove it. Being proactive to reduce the possibility of being victimized by scams, schemes, and identity theft is the best prevention.

Bonus: Know what to do if you are robbed or lose your purse or wallet! Do not delay in taking immediate steps to protect your ID!

New Financial Regulator in Town!

Thanks to Congressional legislation passed in late 2006, the Pentagon is the latest regulator in the financial industry. This new law allows the Pentagon to take steps to protect members of the military service and their families from pay-day loans and other predatory lending services.

The law, which takes effect October 1, 2007, does the following:

- establishes a 36% annual rate cap on interest rates for most loans to military members and their families;
- requires lenders to provide separate and improved information about the loans to military members and their families, and
- sets strict sanctions, including imprisonment, for lenders who violate the law.

Home mortgages, auto loans and credit secured with personal property are exempt from the legislation.

The purpose of the legislation is to shield active duty personnel from lenders who may want to take advantage of families experiencing hardships due to military service.

For more on schemes, scams, and identity theft, complete Backstage Pass on page 89.

CHAPTER SEVEN

HOME SWEET HOME

How many songs can you name that relate to home? With music stars spending so much time on the road, no wonder they sing songs about going home. You can bet celebrities featured on MTV "Cribs" dreamed of their lavish home long before they were famous. Whether it's driving country roads or taking the train to Midtown Manhattan, most of us have some picture of where we want to live and the lifestyle we hope to have.

According to the old real-estate adage, three things give property value—location, location, location! But deciding where to live is only one question to answer. We also need to consider what we can afford and whether we plan to buy or lease. It sounds simple enough, yet it really is more complex than we think. Housing is one of the largest expenditures in our monthly budget and few of us can afford to start out in our dream home. Yet, just closing our eyes and pointing at an ad in the newspaper is not the way to start. As with any other purchases, making informed choices will help us move closer toward our financial goals.

RENTING VERSUS OWNING

Making the decision to rent or purchase a home is more complicated than "paper or plastic" or VCR versus DVD. While the monthly cost is certainly a big consideration, that is not all we have to think about. Some other factors to consider include:

- What is the down payment or deposit?
- What is the length of time we plan to live in the area?
- How much responsibility do we want?
- What is the proximity to school, work, friends, family, public transportation, and other places we frequent?
- How safe is the neighborhood?
- What are the amenities, and will we use them enough to justify paying for them?

RENTING AN APARTMENT

Renting tends to provide a more carefree lifestyle. But that certainly does not imply that we have no responsibility as a renter. In almost every situation we will be asked to sign a lease, which is a legal binding contract that specifies the rights and responsibilities of both the renter and the owner/manager of the apartment. Some of the provisions included in a lease should be the amount of monthly rent, the due date, the length of the lease, what happens if we break a lease, whether or not pets are allowed, plus other stipulations regarding the use of the property.

It is imperative that we read a lease carefully before signing it because we will be held accountable for everything contained in the document. We also want to ensure we keep a copy of the lease after both parties have signed it, in case we need to refer to it to answer questions about our responsibilities. Also, we should inspect the apartment for any damages or safety violations before signing the lease, and any problems should be noted in the lease. Otherwise, we can be held accountable for those problems—costing us hundreds of dollars when we move out. As a backup, its a good idea to take pictures of any damages and date them before moving in—and before showing them to the apartment manager.

Finally, if we are uncomfortable with anything in the apartment, in the complex, or with the management, it is much easier to change our mind before signing the lease.

Breaking a lease can be difficult and costly, so it is best to avoid terminating your contract before the stated end. If we believe that breaking a lease is absolutely necessary, then it's best to refer to our lease for the proper procedures. These provisions can vary significantly from one lease contract to another, but generally a 30-day written notice is required before moving out—even at the end of a lease agreement. Moving out before the lease is over does not end our responsibilities. Unless the lease specifically states otherwise, we are liable for all payments during the lease term whether we live there or not.

Tenant laws are set by the state, meaning they will vary greatly from one state to another. Generally, such tenant laws will spell out the rights of a renter and should be available from the leasing office of any large apartment complex or leasing agent.

Moving into a new area can pose additional problems because it is more difficult to seek advice from friends, family, or colleagues. Most areas have apartment locators or leasing services available to help. However, they may either charge us for their assistance or work only with owners who pay them. Most cities also publish apartment guides or other similar brochures. Even a trip to the local real-estate office or the local chamber of commerce, taking time to surf the Internet, buying a local newspaper, or visiting potential employers may provide information about rental property. When possible, it's a good idea to visit an area on both a weekday and a weekend before making a decision. That provides us with more opportunities to learn about future neighbors and neighborhood. Of course, if friends or family already live in the area, they can be the best source of information.

Once the lease is signed and plans are made to move in, our next visit is to our insurance agent to purchase renter's insurance. Such policies cover theft or damage to our personal property caused by others or by nature. If deadbolt locks are not installed in each door, we probably should ask management about installing them to raise the level of security.

Some leases will allow tenants to paint, replace draperies, or make other minor changes. To be certain, it is safest to ask **before** altering their property. It can also be an expensive mistake if not allowed. Most leases will make allowances for "normal wear and tear," so it's important to understand what is considered to be "normal."

Do you know how much the utilities will run in an apartment or house? Many landlords, gas, or electric companies will provide average bill information for the preceding month if we ask. Knowing what to expect for utilities will help in our decisions to rent because they can vary greatly from one place to another—and from one user to another.

Problems with landlords can arise from time to time. While most deal with late or missed lease payments, others come from privacy matters or unresolved repairs/maintenance issues. A lease should spell out a tenant's privacy rights. If not, the leasing agent should give us a written copy of their policy regarding entering our apartment or making requested repairs. It is also a good idea to know how state law views tenant rights and responsibilities. Virtually all states require owners to provide livable premises, meaning clean, safe, and sanitary conditions with water, heat, and electricity available.

Actions such as refusing to make rent payments or making partial payments to cover required repairs should be taken only with legal counsel. Anything less than full lease payments may lead to eviction or hostility from landlords and could have a negative impact on our credit scores. Renting does not automatically mean livin' easy, but it can be a good option when we take appropriate steps to protect ourselves.

BUYING

Just because the Joneses live in a 5,000-square-foot contemporary home overlooking the beach from the back deck and beautiful mountains from the front balcony doesn't mean we can next door. Buying within our means provides more

---

Did You Know . . .

Under normal circumstances, it takes about five years to recover the initial investment in a home. That means, we would probably lose money when selling our house in the first five years of owning it. Why? Because buying a house is more than making monthly payments. It includes a down payment, closing costs, and other various fees. And that doesn't even take into account the money spent on yard work, repairs, and maintenance.

peace and relaxation than any beach or mountaintop. Owning a home is a long-term investment that has a relatively high level of risk. While the value of real estate tends to appreciate over time, there are **no** guarantees. Any house or property is only worth what someone is willing to pay us when we are ready to sell.

The advantage of owning is that we have the opportunity to build equity. Because real estate is an investment, we can turn a potential profit on it. Also, it is ours. No more worries about whether the apartment manager will complain about the lime paint in the living room or the shocking pink, flowered wallpaper in the bath. We are in charge! At the same time, we need to think about measures that will protect the value of our property. Tearing out walls to make the greatest, grandest master bedroom suite may sound like fun, but how many people are in the market for a one-bedroom house designed like a private castle?

Most of us seek assistance from a licensed real-estate agent when looking for a house to buy. Real-estate agents and brokers are excellent resources for learning about a new area or introducing us to new neighborhoods. When purchasing a home or property, the real-estate agent is generally paid by the seller—even when we go to them for help making the purchase.

We may also want to visit a financial institution to go through the prequalification process to determine how much house we can afford. Prequalifying means the lender has given us a firm commitment to loan us a certain amount of money even though we haven't found the specific house. Taking the time to prequalify helps us focus in on specific prices ranges and reduce the amount of time needed to process loan papers after we sign a contract. In addition, prequalifying shows the real-estate agent and potential sellers that we are serious about making a deal and may give us an advantage when negotiating the final price.

However, just because we can QUALIFY for a certain payment doesn't mean we should pay that much or that we should buy a larger house. Larger, more expensive homes may result in higher property taxes, higher utility bills, higher insurance premiums, and even higher maintenance and repair costs.

Qualifying for a loan is based primarily on our credit report. The better our credit score, the lower the interest rate. Poor credit can be costly, even to the point of being denied a loan. (Note: We can also be turned down by a leasing agent if our scores are too low—meaning we have few options for finding a place to live independently.) If this happens, we have a couple of options: delay our home purchase until we have improved our credit or find someone to co-sign a loan for us. When getting a co-signer, it is imperative that we are absolutely sure we can make those monthly payments on time. It is not in our best interest or fair to our co-signer to make late payments or stop making them. Such actions further damage our credit and can destroy the credit rating for the co-signer who was only trying to help us.

Generally, buying a home requires us to make a down payment. If we can afford a down payment equal to or more than 20 percent of the cost of the house, then we will not be required to purchase Private Mortgage Insurance (PMI). PMI ensures the lender that we will make our payments or protect the lender in case we default on our loan. After our loan principal drops below 80 percent of the total value of our home, then we can stop paying PMI—which decreases our monthly payment by that amount.

When buying a house today, there are many options for financing. Comparison shopping for loans is even more important than shopping around for the best price on a new television or car. Even a half percent difference on a home or car loan can save us thousands of dollars.

And we need to remember to check out the points and other costs associated with getting a housing loan because they vary from lender to lender. Different financial institutions offer different financing options, which can get confusing unless we ask lots of questions. We should expect to find lower interest rates as the amount of down payment increases. Sometimes there are special programs offering little or no down payment for first-time home buyers or other targeted groups, but most of us can expect to put down between 3 percent and 20 percent when buying a home.

It is not advisable to drain our savings just for the down payment because we will need additional money to complete the deal. Additional funds will be needed for the various fees called closing costs as well as money to pay for the move, deposits on utilities, and other costs associated with moving. Having a little extra will certainly reduce the stress and keep us from pulling out those credit cards. (Note: Go to *http://www.hud.gov/utilities/intercept.cfm?/buying/booklet.pdf* to download a publication called *Looking for the Best Mortgage* for more information, including a mortgage comparison guide.)

The Fair Housing Act prohibits discrimination based on race, color, religion, national origin, handicap, sex, and familial status in all residential real-estate purchases. According to this law, we cannot be refused a loan or charged a higher interest rate based solely on these characteristics.

Whether leasing or buying, finding a place to live should not be a "snap" decision. Taking some time and effort can greatly improve our chances of making a good choice and keep us on track for meeting our financial goals.

In many cases, the amount of money a renter spends on rent can be about the same as or less than the amount a homeowner spends on a mortgage. With the tax benefit for homeowners, the savings can be significant.

BUYING VERSUS RENTING COMPARISON

The above chart shows a cost comparison for a renter and a homeowner over a seven-year period.

The renter starts out paying $800 per month with annual increases of 5 percent.

The homeowner purchases a home for $110,000 and pays a monthly mortgage of $1,000.

After **six** years, the **homeowner's payment** is **lower** than the renter's monthly payment.

With the tax savings of homeownership, the **homeowner's payment** is **less** than the rental payment after **three** years.

RENTING VERSUS BUYING

Years	Rent Payment	Mortgage Payment	Monthly Difference	After-Tax Savings	Yearly Difference	After-Tax Savings
1	800	1000	−200	−50	−2400	−600
2	840	1000	−160	−10	−1920	−120
3	882	1000	−118	+32	−1416	+384
4	926	1000	−74	+76	−888	+912
5	972	1000	−28	+122	−336	+1464
6	1021	1000	+21	+171	+252	+2052
7	1072	1000	+72	+222	+864	+2664
8–30				*Savings increase every year*		

MONTHLY EXPENSES: BUYING

Your rental company takes part of your rent payment to cover certain housing expenses. When you decide to purchase a home, you accept responsibility for paying for these expenses (listed on the next page). They are additional costs to your monthly mortgage payment and should be included in your budget estimates:

Property Taxes and Special Assessments

Home/Hazard Insurance

Utilities

Maintenance

Home Owner Association (HOA) Fee: Doesn't apply to all purchases. It pays for trash and snow removal and maintenance of common grounds if applicable.

Membership Fee: It may pay for recreational facilities and other services (cable TV).

Source: *http://www.ginniemae.gov/rent_vs_buy/rent_vs_buy_chart.asp?section=YPTH.*

LIVIN' LARGE: HOUSING TIPS

1. Ask questions. If "location, location, location" gives property its value, then "questions, questions, questions" give us the information we need to wisely evaluate our housing needs and to make an informed selection.

2. Know what you can afford and stick with it. Even when friends, family members, leasing agents, real-estate agents, and others think they are helping by encouraging us to get something "nicer" or "larger," be sure you can afford to pay for their suggestions without busting your budget. After all, you don't want to spend everything on just a place to live.

3. Find qualified agents to help. Whether buying or selling, be sure you turn to qualified professionals who are willing to help you meet your goals. Those more interested in their fees than in your needs are not a good choice.

4. Keep your credit healthy. Having a good credit history and high credit scores will save you money on a home mortgage and on your property insurance. Overloading with debt lowers your score and reduces your options for housing.

5. Make decisions with your head and not your heart. Choosing a place to live just because it's cute or cool is an emotion choice, and emotion choices generally cost us more money in the long run. Being sensible and practical with our housing decisions pays off now and later.

6. Inspect before signing. Whether buying a house or leasing an apartment, be sure you inspect it carefully for damages or needed repairs. With a lease, you can be held liable for those damages if you don't report them to management before signing the lease. With a house, you will want to hire a qualified home inspector before closing. Anything you want repaired before moving in needs to be put in writing.

7. Prepare for the hunt. "Doing your homework" in this case means even more than completing your assignment for class. Researching neighborhoods, finding professional agents, shopping for interest rates, prequalifying for loans, and other work behind the scenes prepares you to start looking.

8. Remember to get insurance. Going without insurance on your personal belongings in an apartment or on your home is like playing with matches— eventually, you will get burned. It's really a small price to pay for the additional peace of mind.

9. Read everything carefully before you sign. Signing a lease, making an offer on a home, and signing loan papers or any other agreements are legal contracts.

Need a Roommate?

At some point, you may decide to have a roommate to help share expenses. That's a great way to live in a nicer area or larger apartment, and generally half the rent for a larger apartment is still less than paying for a small apartment by yourself. So, how do you find a roommate?

- You probably first think of your best friend, but remember, best friends don't always make the best roommates. Before you decide, stop and think about that friend's habits. What annoys you the most? Is it something you can put up with every day, for extended periods of time?

- You may want to post an ad or look through classified ads. If you chose to take this route, be sure you take time to interview the person. You may even want to pay to have a background check. It's better to be safe than sorry.

Will It Work?

One of the keys to having a successful roomie relationship is setting some ground rules before you sign a lease. Discuss what is acceptable and what is not. Establish quiet time hours. Determine how rent and utilities will be divided. And, talk about sharing costs for food, cleaning supplies, and so on.

Regardless of whom you select, you will need to stay flexible and accepting of differences. Living with someone can be challenging, but fun. And it's a great way to save money on housing.

Choosing a Real-Estate Agent

Finding a qualified real-estate specialist to assist with your house-hunting can make things much easier—while working with someone not so qualified can be a nightmare. Following are some suggestions to consider when making the selection:

- Ask for references from friends or family.

- Look for someone with at least two years' experience who is working full-time in the profession.

- Check out their credentials. In addition to a state license, many professional real-estate agents will have a GRI designation, meaning they are a graduate of the Realtors® Institute.

- Talk to more than one person before deciding; you want someone interested in your needs and with whom you are comfortable sharing personal information. Remember, you may be spending a lot of time with this person during your search.

- Be sure they will answer your questions and consider what is in your best interest.

And all legal contracts are binding. In other words, you will be held account-able for anything in those contracts—even if you don't understand what they say. So ask questions and be sure you know exactly what your rights and responsibilities are before signing.

10. Put everything in writing. Don't rely on verbal agreements; they are not legally binding because it is your word against theirs. If the apartment manager promises to replace your locks or replace the carpet, get it in writing. If the person selling your house says they will include the refrigerator or repair the roof, get it in writing. Even honest people can have short memories, so the written word is a nice, gentle reminder.

For more on renting an apartment, complete Backstage Pass on page 91.

CHAPTER EIGHT

INSURANCE

Famous entertainers have insured everything from noses to legs to protect their potential loss of income resulting from damage or injury to those specific body parts.

Few of us would consider purchasing insurance on our smile, teeth, nose, or legs. But most of us will purchase insurance on a car or home—as well as some type of life or health insurance.

Insurance plays a role in our ability to manage our personal wealth. It helps us repair or replace things we own that are damaged, lost, or destroyed, which can be rather expensive to do. It also helps us cover any short-term or long-term losses of income and provides a safety net to help cover many of the risks we face daily. Without an appropriate level of insurance, our wealth can be wiped out in a short period of time. At the same time, we need to be cautious about buying more insurance than we need or paying more than we should. Insurance is a necessary and valuable financial resource, and that's why this chapter is included in a book about money.

Basically, insurance transfers our risk to an insurance company, and we pay them to absorb that risk for us. The companies take that risk and spread it over the many people who are paying them premiums for coverage. Having insurance is different from most purchases because we are buying something we hope we never have to use! And they are selling something without really knowing exactly how much it will cost them or how often they will need to pay us. The companies are also predicting that only a few of us in their pool will actually experience a loss, allowing them to offer each of us a reduced cost for the insurance.

The level of risk has a great impact on the insurance premiums you pay. The higher the risk, the higher the insurance premiums will be. Risk managers and insurance professionals must keep up with the rapid changes in the marketplace as well as changes in social behaviors. For example, no one was talking about banning cell phones while driving ten years ago. Today, however, it is a hot topic among policymakers. Whether we agree or disagree with the risk involved in talking on the phone while driving, few can question that it has set off a hot debate in many cities around the country.

The insurance industry is divided into two primary areas: life/health insurance and property/casualty insurance. Some companies specialize in

one or the other, but most large insurance companies offer both. All types of insurance are regulated by a state insurance department, and each state has its own set of rules for companies selling in their state. Property/casualty insurance policies tend to be more highly regulated because the level of coverage is often mandated by state law or required by some other entity, such as a bank or lender.

It is our responsibility to know any mandated level of coverage in the state in which we live, and to maintain level of insurance. We can always choose to exceed the requirement, but it is not a good decision to purchase less. Even though it is tempting to buy less than we need or are required to have in order to save money, it is certain to cost us much more in the long run. In today's world, some forms of insurance are necessities, not luxuries. So, be sure you included your insurance premiums in your monthly spending plan and that you make those payments!

Knowing the required amounts of insurance and determining our ability to manage future losses helps us assess our individual insurance needs. Following are a few questions to get us started:

1. What kind of auto insurance is required in my state?
2. If you have a loan on your car or a home, what kind of insurance does your lender require?
3. What types of insurance are "must haves" and which are not really necessary?
4. How much insurance do you really need to purchase?
5. How do you find the best deal on insurance?
6. Are all insurance companies the same or do they all charge the same fees?

Our state insurance department or the contract we signed when making our purchase should be able to provide answers to the first two questions.

Did You Know . . .

Insurance costs (generally called premiums) can vary greatly from one company to the next. Take time to call more than one local insurance broker to compare prices and coverage options. You may also want to use the Internet to gather information or get price comparisons. Before starting, be sure you have all the information needed for insurances agents to respond to your request. For example, if you are comparing the price of car insurance, you will need information on your driving record, the type of car you drive, the car's age and VIN number, your grades, the type of coverage you want, and so forth. They may even want to review your credit report before giving you a price quote. (Many companies give discounts for good credit scores and good grades!)

While price is important, remember it is only one factor to consider before buying an insurance policy.

Also, be sure you get all quotes in writing so you can better compare them before making a choice.

To help answer these questions, we probably want to consult a trusted professional insurance specialist. Finding an insurance agent more interested in our financial future than just selling us a policy can be invaluable when evaluating our insurance needs. A qualified agent will take time to know us and our special needs before making recommendations or selling us a product. The agent should ask several questions about our background and be able to answer any questions that we have. Because any good relationship has a flip side, we must be open and honest with them—just like we expect them to be upfront with us. It is difficult for an agent to act in our best interest when we have withheld information from them. We also need to have a periodic review of our insurance needs, especially if we have any life changes such as marriage, divorce, a new baby, and so on. An annual review will help minimize our risk and better protect our financial resources.

Just as all agents are not the same, all companies and all policies are not the same. A.M. Best is one of the top sources of information about insurance companies. Best is a worldwide agency devoted to issuing in-depth reports and financial ratings of insurance organizations. These ratings give us information about a company's solvency based on a comprehensive review of its balance sheet, operating performance, and business profile. While Best ratings do not guarantee the insurer can meet all of its financial obligations to us, it remains one of the more reliable resources about an insurance company's financial health. Because insurance companies are not "insured" or "guaranteed" by the government, the financial strength of an individual company is one of the best indicators we can use to when selecting someone to help protect our financial futures. Visit *http://www.ambest.com* for more information.

DO WE NEED . . .

Property Insurance

A home is the most expensive purchase most of us will make during our lifetime and it's frequently our most valuable asset. Consider what would happen if we suddenly lost it because of fire or weather. Or, what if the contents were stolen or damaged? How would we pay to replace them? Or, what if someone sues us for an injury caused by tripping over a bike in our yard or falls down our stairs? These are just some of the reasons to buy homeowner's insurance.

But what if we just rent? Can we afford to replace everything we have if the apartment burns or is ransacked? What if a neighbor's water pipe bursts and floods our apartment? While landlords insure the apartment building against damage, their insurance policy does not cover our belongings. Most of us would agree that it would be financially difficult to replace clothing, computers, and other personal property after a disaster. Therefore, investing in an apartment renter's policy is probably in our best interest. Hopefully, we never need to use it. But at least we have financial assistance when we do.

Health or Medical Insurance

What happens if we become sick or disabled, temporarily or permanently? Would we be able to pay all of the costs and still support ourselves? Probably not. **Health** insurance will help offset our medical-related costs while **disability** insurance provides us with some form of income should we become unable to work for extended periods of time. Medical costs and disruptions in income are two of the leading reasons that many families file for bankruptcy today, which means we need to carefully consider our options when making decisions about health insurance.

Health insurance is often one of our employee benefits, especially in professional positions. Most companies offer a selection of health or medical insurance with different levels of costs and benefits. It is very important for us to review the different options and ask lots of questions before signing up. Making an uninformed decision or a wild guess about what's best can be a very costly choice!

Life Insurance

Life insurance is an interesting purchase. It's something we buy for someone else to have the benefit after we're no longer living. Most people need some kind of life insurance, but how much and what type is debatable. To answer those questions, we can think about it this way: If we died tomorrow, what would our family members or loved ones need to survive financially? While money won't replace an individual, it can help those left pay any expenses resulting from our death without incurring additional financial hardships.

Maybe this will help make an unemotional decision about the amount needed:

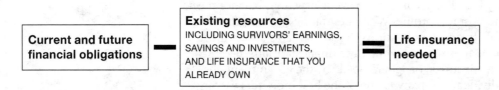

Source: http://www.life-line.org (Life and Health Insurance Foundation for Education)
Note: This website also includes a life insurance needs calculator to help in the decision.

Life insurance comes in many different forms, but is generally divided into two large groups: term and permanent. **Term insurance** is a less expensive form of insurance designed to meet temporary needs. It lasts for a specific period of time, has a declining value, and pays off only during that time. **Permanent insurance** provides life-long coverage, as long as the premiums are paid. It tends to cost more than term insurance but does accumulate some cash value in addition to paying the full amount of the policy. Decisions about what kind of life insurance is best for us should be made after consulting with a qualified life insurance professional.

Long-Term Care Insurance

No one wants to think about long-term care—at least not until we need it. But needing perpetual care in a facility or at home can wreck our finances in a few months. Full-time nursing home care can run as much as $60,000 a year, and there aren't too many people who can afford that. Long-term care is not just for the aged. In fact, a growing number of young people are requiring special care as a result of car accidents or debilitating illnesses. Buying a long-term policy is much less expensive when we are young than when we are older. However, not everyone can afford it. Industry experts say that a good rule of thumb is spending no more than 7 percent of our gross income on long-term-care insurance premiums.

Auto Insurance

An auto insurance policy is a package of different kinds of insurance coverages including collision, liability, medical, and others. While most states require a minimum amount of certain kinds, most of us will want to purchase a sufficient amount to protect us from potential lawsuits or repair bills. **Liability** is the basis of auto insurance. It pays for bodily injury and property damage caused to others in an accident, as well as any legal bills resulting from it. Liability coverage limits (for the damage we do to others) are usually a series of three numbers, such as 30/40/20. That stands for $30,000 in bodily injury coverage per person, $40,000 in bodily injury per accident, and $20,000 in property-damage coverage per accident.

When we are responsible for the accident, the repairs to our vehicle are covered by **collision** insurance. As a general rule, we cannot collect more than the actual cash value of our car—which is not the same as the replacement cost. Collision coverage tends to be the most expensive part of our policy. We can reduce the cost by choosing a higher deductible, such as $500 or $1,000. This means that we must pay that amount before the insurance company will pay the rest. It is important to keep the amount needed for our deductible in one of our savings or investment accounts.

Other types of insurance included the following:

- **Medical payments** cover our medical expenses along with those incurred by any passengers in our vehicle. These expenses may result when we are driving our own car, someone else's car (with their permission!), or injuries we suffer as a pedestrian.
- **Personal injury protection** (PIP) is an expanded form of medical payments and may even cover expenses such as lost wages and child care. Such expanded coverages may not be necessary if they are part of our health or disability insurance plans.
- **Uninsured motorists** (UM) clauses pay for injuries suffered by a hit-and-run driver or someone who doesn't have auto insurance. In some states, it will also pay for any related property damage. It is required in many states.
- **Rental reimbursement** covers car rental fees when our vehicle is too damaged to drive or stolen.
- **Towing and labor** pays for any charges we incur from breaking down on the highway.
- **Gap coverage** is used to pay the difference between the actual cash value we receive for the car and the amount left on our car loan if the vehicle is totaled in an accident. Some lending institutions require gap insurance as part of the terms of the loan.

Most of us are somewhat familiar with these types of insurances. However, there are others. Here is a list of other types of insurance coverage we may encounter:

Insurance Tip

If the deductible is more than the cost of the repairs, it is better to just pay the bill and not report the claim to the insurance company. This practice will save money in the long run because the number of claims filed is computed into our premium.

To check out a potential insurance agent or company:

Consumer Reports—a magazine that frequently includes articles on insurance.

Better Business Bureau—a good place to check out the number of complaints filed against a local agent in your area.

A. M. Best—a widely recognized reviewer of insurance companies.

Standard and Poor's—another group that rates the financial health of insurance companies.

www.insure.com—a reliable source of information on all companies selling insurance in your state.

Insurance company websites—while not always impartial, many insurance companies have excellent websites with information on local agents, their company ratings, and general tips on purchasing insurance.

Replacement Cost versus Actual Cash Value

Replacement cost is the amount needed to replace a vehicle or repair damages with materials of similar kind and quality, without deducting for depreciation. Depreciation is the decrease in vehicle value because of age or wear and tear.

Actual cash value (ACV) is the value of your property when it is damaged or destroyed. Claims adjusters usually figure ACV by taking the replacement cost and subtracting depreciation.

- Be sure they will answer your questions and consider what is in your best interest.

Mortgage Life Insurance: Pays off a home mortgage in case the policyholder (the person making the mortgage payments) dies before the house is paid off. Mortgage life insurance is one of the most expensive insurances we can purchase. Instead, we can purchase a decreasing term-life insurance for much less that provides the same benefits.

Credit Card Balance Insurance: Makes payments on a credit card balance if we become unemployed, disabled, or die. This kind of insurance is also very expensive and tends to cost more than it is worth.

Lost or Stolen Credit Card Insurance: Covers the first $50 of charges if our cards are lost or stolen. Under federal law, we are not responsible for charges over $50 and insurance to cover that initial $50 is very expensive.

Flight Insurance: Pays benefits to our family if we are injured or killed in an airline accident. If we have health and life insurance, there is no good reason to pay high premiums for special coverages like this one.

Myth

I don't need long-term-care insurance because the government will pay for my care should I ever need it.

Reality

Medicaid, the government's long-term-care program for low-income Americans, only kicks in after your own assets are significantly depleted and there's little left over for your spouse or family. Relying on Medicaid may also make it harder to find the type of care or facility that's most convenient for you.

Source: http://www.life-line.org (Life and Health Insurance Foundation for Education).

Travel Insurance: Pays medical benefits when we are traveling outside the "network" coverage or when traveling internationally, including the cost of transporting us home for medical reason. Depending upon our situation, we may want to consider it—but only when absolutely necessary.

Trip Cancellation Insurance: Allows us to be reimbursed for prepaid travel arrangements that need to be cancelled due to last-minute changes, whether medical or personal. Most will also reimburse us if the travel agent or tour operator files bankruptcy before the trip is completed. This type of insurance can be helpful when budgets are tight—but we need to be sure the benefits outweigh our costs.

Private Mortgage Insurance (PMI): An extra insurance that lenders require from most homebuyers who obtain loans that are more than 80 percent of their new home's value. In other words, buyers with less than a 20 percent down payment are normally required to pay PMI as part of their monthly payments. The good news is that it allows us to buy a home with less money down, but it does increase our monthly payment. According to the Homeowner's Protection Act, buyers have the right to request cancellation of PMI when we pay down our mortgage to the point that it equals 80 percent of the original purchase price or the appraised value of our home at the time the loan was obtained, whichever is less.

In case we haven't figured it out, there is someone willing to insure about anything we're willing to pay to have insured. But that doesn't make it necessary. Buying unneeded insurance can be very expensive and negatively impact our finances. Before buying any kind of insurance, it is important to know what we are buying and why we are buying it. Remember, insurance salespeople are always ready to sell because that's how they make a living. But a qualified insurance professional is much more likely to recommend only what is in our best financial interest.

LIVIN' LARGE: INSURANCE TIPS

1. Before making a decision about insurance, shop around! Take time to find out your alternatives because not all insurance is the same and not all insurance costs the same. Policy provisions and premiums for the provisions vary greatly from one company to another, and there is no reason to pay more than necessary for insurance coverage. Thanks to the Internet, shopping is even easier. (Warning: Be careful about giving too much personal information online or to someone who calls offering you discounted insurance.)

2. Improve your credit scores and credit history. Yes, individuals with higher credit scores pay less for insurance than those with low credit scores and a poor payment history. Why? Low scores equal high risk—and insurance companies must charge enough to cover their risk. Paying your bills on time and maintaining a good credit rating will lower insurance costs and save you money.

3. Increase your deductible. While low deductibles are nice, they are also expensive. You may be able to reduce your home and auto premiums by 10 percent or more when you raise your deductibles. Put the difference in your savings

Take a Home Inventory

Having an up-to-date home inventory will help you:

- Purchase enough insurance to replace the things you own.
- Get your insurance claims settled faster.
- Substantiate losses for your income tax return.

You can always simply make a list in a notebook and save receipts and photos in a file, or find reliable software to help make this task fun and simple—and easy to update as you buy or eliminate personal possessions.

Getting Started

If you have been setting up a household, starting a home inventory can be relatively simple. You could even attach recent wedding registries to substantiate new possessions. But, if you have been living in a house for many years, this task may seem daunting. If you set aside an afternoon and get your entire household involved, it can be an enjoyable experience. It is much easier to document your possessions before you suffer a loss from a fire, hurricane, burglary, or other disaster.

Big-Ticket Items

Make note of expensive items, such as jewelry, furs, and collectibles. Valuable items may need separate insurance. But, don't forget more common-place items such as toys, CDs, and clothing.

Taking Photographs

Along with the written information, consider adding photographs of your possessions, which can be done easily with a digital camera. Those with film cameras can scan print photographs or have their film developer save the images to a disk. You can always simply store your print photographs with a copy of your inventory.

Videotape It

Walk through your house or apartment videotaping the contents. Remember to open drawers and closets. One advantage of videotape is that you can narrate what you are filming. Visit http://www.iii.org/ to download free home inventory software. Find a safe place to store your videotape and records, such as a safety deposit box. You might also give a copy to a trustworthy family member so it will be stored elsewhere in case of a major disaster or emergency.

Source: *http://www.iii.org*, the Insurance Information Institute.

account so you have the money available, just in case it's needed. Any savings can be "eaten up" by charging your deductible to a credit card and paying interest on it.

4. Review your policies annually. Life happens. And any life change means you need to review your financial management strategies—including insurance. Should you decide to make a change, never cancel an existing policy until the new one has been written.

5. Ask about discounts. Insurance companies generally offer a variety of discounts to their customers or potential customers. For example, you may be able to reduce auto premiums if you recently attended a driver's training course or if you make good grades. Also, insurance companies will generally discount prices if you buy more than one policy from them (such as a car insurance policy and an apartment insurance policy).

6. Be honest. When completing insurance applications or checking prices, don't give false or misleading information. If you smoke, fess up. If you had an accident, give 'em details. By hiding information, you may end up paying more than expected, having your application rejected, or, even worse, having your insurance policy cancelled.

7. Determine if you need special coverage. If you have expensive stereo equipment in your apartment or your car, you may need a special "endorsement" to cover the replacement cost. Keep in mind that endorsements will increase your premiums. So, be sure the additional benefits are more than the additional cost.

8. Take steps to protect your property. Just buying insurance does not release your responsibility. Install safety, antitheft, or tracking devices on your personal property. Don't leave your keys in your car or your front door—and be sure to lock doors on cars and homes. You may even need to consider moving if living in a high-risk neighborhood. An insurance company may decide not to pay for stolen items if you have not taken steps to secure them. While we don't want to be paranoid, we have to realize we increase our risk of having a car stolen if we leave it running while we go in the convenience store—and increasing our risk will eventually increase our premiums.

9. Don't just buy the basics. Consider YOUR insurance needs, not what the state or a contract requires. Just the basics may or may not be in your best interest.

10. Cost is only one consideration. Establishing a good relationship with an insurance professional and paying premiums to a reliable company are more important than getting a bargain. Customer service, financial stability, licensed agents, and concern for your future will pay off.

For more on insurance, complete Backstage Pass on pages 93–94.

CHAPTER NINE
SAVINGS AND INVESTING

Nothing ventured, nothing gained. How many times have we heard that?

How much we are willing to venture certainly does correlate with what we gain, but it doesn't mean that we should dive in without thinking about the depth of the water.

When musicians or writers set out to create the perfect hit record, they have some idea about what they like, what others like, and what will sell. Otherwise, they run the risk of being a "one-hit wonder" or a "never was."

Taking a risk is part of life. We take a risk getting out of bed each morning, and may assume other risks if we don't. The same is true when it comes to saving and investing. Putting money away for the future offers few, if any, guarantees. But we are guaranteed to get "nothing" unless we take the steps to save and invest for our financial goals.

Savings is basically setting money aside in our monthly budget to meet short-term goals. Savings includes an emergency fund for those "just in case" times that seem to come along more often than we wish. Think about the most expensive unplanned purchase you've made in the last three or four years. Did you replace the water pump on a car, have to replace a library or textbook, buy a new washer when the old one died, or repair a leak in the roof after a good thunderstorm? That is a good gauge for the amount of money needed in an emergency account. While some professional money managers prefer two to three months of income in that account, we may not want to put that much into a low-interest-bearing account—especially as a young investor. Money in a savings account should draw interest while also being liquid—meaning we can easily get our hands on it to make purchases. But if the interest earned is less than the rate of inflation, we are actually losing money because our purchasing power is decreasing.

Most savings accounts today have very low interest rates, so many financial advisors encourage people to put their emergency funds into a money market account. Money market accounts at a bank, savings and loan, or credit union are insured by the federal government, providing savers with only a miniscule amount of risk. While we certainly won't get rich quick with a money market account, our money is insured and very easy to access when we *need* it.

Money markets are a good option for emergency fund accounts. However, we probably want to look at ways to earn a greater return on our money. Many people today use mutual funds because they have a professional manager who is responsible for investing the money and managing the account. With a mutual fund, we buy a share of the fund, lowering our cost of investing.

Two words can really make a huge impact on our future: consistency and diversification. When starting a savings or investing plan, our results will be much greater if we remember to save or invest consistently and if we diversify our portfolio.

Even when living on a very limited income, we should be able to find a few dollars each month to put away into savings. Once we make the commitment to save, it is important to save consistently and to leave the money in our account until needed for a REAL emergency. Buying pizza at midnight or a shoe sale do not qualify as emergencies!

Starting to save as a young adult has amazing results because of compounding. Compounding interest on savings works in our favor—while compounding interest on our debt works against us. Have you ever wondered how long it would take you to save a certain amount or double your original investment, or pay off a certain amount? It really depends on the interest rate, or rate of return we will receive on our money. The "Rule of 72" can help answer that question. Basically, this rule means that money will double every 7.2 years at 10 percent interest. So, what if we can't get 10 percent or we want our money to double faster? Here's how we can use the Rule of 72 to make those estimates:

Rule of 72

Divide 72 by the interest rate to get the number of years needed to double the money. For example, $1,000 in savings at 6 percent interest: 72/6 = 12. If we don't add an additional amount to our savings, we will have $2,000 in 12 years.

What if we want it to double in five years? 72/5=14.4. We would need an investment paying 14.4 percent to have $2,000 in five years.

Does that sound impossible? Maybe not. Stocks in the United States have had an average rate of return of 12 to 14 percent annually since the inception of the stock markets. But keep in mind, that's average—meaning some years have been MUCH less and other years have been higher. Investments in stocks have no guaranteed returns and tend to be more successful when invested for a longer period of time, so we need to think carefully before purchasing stocks to meet short-term needs.

The Rule of 72 is amazingly accurate as long as we are using interest rates of less than 20 percent. In fact, Albert Einstein called it the "greatest mathematical discovery of all time."

(Note: With debt, the Rule of 72 estimates the length of time needed for your debt to double at various interest rates. In other words, the balance on a credit card will double in 7.2 years when paying 10 percent interest.)

Diversification reinforces Grandma's advice, "Don't put all your eggs in one basket!" In monetary terms, it means that our investment portfolio should include several different strategies. Having a diversified portfolio is more than just buying stocks from different companies or buying a variety of stocks and bonds. It includes examining the way Uncle Sam views the different types of investment

options. "Uploading" more than one strategy provides protection when we actually need to use the money, not just when we establish the account.

When establishing an investment plan, consider having four different investment accounts. Think of them as four different songs on your wealth CD:

- **"Oh Brother, Another Emergency"** by Needing Cash
- **"Maxin' Out My 401k"** by Planning Smart
- **"Where's My Roth?"** by Building Wealth
- **"Life Happens"** by Protecting Futures

"OH BROTHER, ANOTHER EMERGENCY"

That's our emergency savings account, and, yes, everyone needs an emergency fund. Because it is liquid, we can easily access the cash instead of relying on credit to make needed car repairs or replace the air conditioning in our home. If this is our only savings account, we probably want to have a little more cushion—adding a minimum of three months' salary. Shopping around to find the best interest rate may bring

So you can't save or don't know where to start? One of the easiest ways to start saving is to have a certain amount automatically withdrawn from your checking account or paycheck each month. Stashing away money before you even see it reduces the potential of failing to pay yourself and increases the potential of saving consistently.

Another option is setting a jar by the bed and dropping all your change in it each night before you go to bed. Take that money to the bank at the end of each month and you'll be surprised how much you can save.

Do you shop with coupons? Add the savings from your purchases to the nightly change jar and it will grow even faster. The same idea works at fast-food places. Instead of "supersizing" your purchase, buy the regular size and drop the additional amount in your glove compartment. Add it to the change in your jar before going to the bank each month.

surprising results. Not all interest rates on savings accounts, money markets, or other savings tools are the same, whether looking at banks or other financial institutions. Before starting, however, we need to be comfortable with the past and potential future earnings of the organization before placing our money in their care.

"MAXIN' OUT"

Many employers provide 401k or similar retirement plans. Generally a company will either contribute a certain percentage of our income or match a maximum percentage of what we pay into the account. Called self-directed retirement accounts, tools such as a 401k are established under the IRS Code (that's where the numbers come from!) and allow us to make choices about how we invest the money paid in. Companies contract with a financial institution that gives us a menu of options to help in making our selection.

Income paid into these types of retirement accounts is pretaxed. In other words, we do not pay income tax on it at the time we earn the money. We will, however, pay income tax on the amount we withdraw after age 59 1/2. Taking it out before then results in paying the current rate of income tax plus a 10 percent penalty. Currently, Uncle Sam also requires us to start withdrawing from our 401ks at age 70—whether we need the money or not.

Here are some tips to remember when setting up a self-directed retirement account:

- Review the available choices carefully before deciding how to allot your money, realizing that you will have the opportunity to make changes at a future point in time.

- Put as much into the account as needed to get the company's full match; otherwise, you are leaving free money on the table. For example, if the company's plan will match up to 6 percent of your salary, you should put 6 percent of your salary into the account to get the full match.

- Younger people can afford to take more risk than persons approaching retirement. Investing the majority of your retirement in moderate to high-risk stocks is a risk you can afford to take when starting out. However, someone expecting to retire in the next 5 to 10 years may want to shift those funds to something with low to moderate risk. Why? A young person won't need that

---

Did You Know . . .

How much does a cup of coffee cost you?

Would you believe $465.84? Or more?

If you buy a cup of coffee every day for $1.00 (an awfully good price for a decent cup of coffee, nowadays), that adds up to $365.00 a year. If you saved that $365.00 for just 1 year, and put it into a savings account or investment that earns 5 percent a year, it would grow to $465.84 by the end of 5 years, and by the end of 30 years, to $1,577.50.

That's the power of "compounding." With compound interest, you earn interest on the money you save and on the interest that money earns. Over time, even a small amount saved can add up to big money. If you are willing to watch what you spend and look for little ways to save on a regular schedule, you can make money grow. You just did it with one cup of coffee.

If a small cup of coffee can make such a huge difference, start looking at how you could make your money grow if you decided to spend less on other things and save those extra dollars.

Source: Get the Facts: The SEC's Roadmap to Saving and Investing, http://www.sec.gov/investor/pubs/roadmap.htm.

---

money for several years and can recover from any losses; recovering that money is much more difficult for someone who will need the money to live on in a few years.

- Diversify your account by including domestic, foreign, and global stocks and bonds, as well as a variety of high-, moderate-, and low-risk funds. Unless we have a worldwide recession, investing in business around the world provides an investment cushion and the difference in risk helps balance your investment.

- Review your monthly or quarterly statements to track the performance of your investment. Some declines are expected and should not be alarming. If you have questions, however, be sure to ask a trusted financial advisor.

Depending on your income and employment status, a traditional IRA (Individual Retirement Account) has some of the same characteristics as a 401(k) or other employer retirement accounts. Money placed in these accounts postpones our responsibility to pay income tax on the amount invested until time to withdraw it. In addition, the IRS requires us to start drawing down those funds at age 59 1/2 and we suffer penalties for early withdrawal.

Uploading our 401(k) or other employer-sponsored retirement accounts is a "must have." And if we're self-employed, we can invest in a government-qualified plan designed especially for us.

"WHERE'S MY ROTH?"

The Roth IRA is a different approach to retirement planning. We pay income tax on the money put into a Roth and can then withdraw it, starting at age 59 1/2, tax-free. And, like any other investment opportunity, we should contribute the maximum amount possible. Why a separate Roth IRA when we have a 401(k) or a traditional IRA? The Roth gives us a different strategy for managing our income tax responsibilities by paying it now instead of guessing what the rate will be when we retire, and all earnings in the account can also be withdrawn tax-free.

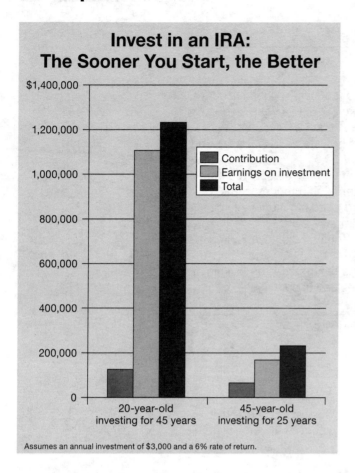

Invest in an IRA: The Sooner You Start, the Better

Legend:
- Contribution
- Earnings on investment
- Total

X-axis categories:
- 20-year-old investing for 45 years
- 45-year-old investing for 25 years

Assumes an annual investment of $3,000 and a 6% rate of return.

Roth accounts are best for savers who anticipate having significant amounts of taxable income in their retirement years. They are rarely matched by employers, so we're better off using them after "maxing out" our 401K contributions.

"LIFE HAPPENS"

Establishing a "Life Happens" account puts us in greater control of our financial future. Finding an investment option that maximizes its earning potential and remains somewhat liquid will round out an ideal financial plan. Because Uncle Sam regulates what we can and cannot do with most of our retirement funds, having an additional account that we manage along with a professional advisor gives us greater flexibility and more options in how we spend our money and when we withdraw it.

Mutual funds are one of the most recommended options for this type of investment for people who have limited time, money, or knowledge about investing because mutual funds have a professional manager and generally offer a diversified pool of investment tools. Mutual funds are also rather liquid, allowing immediate access to our investment. A "Life Happens" account may seem like a luxury we cannot afford, but it is something to consider when drafting our spending plans and building sufficient wealth to achieve our financial goals. It's also a great place to stash that "cushion" of three months' minimum salary because we would expect having a greater rate of return on this account than on our "Oh Brother, Another Emergency" account.

(Note: This chapter is intended to provide basic information on the different types of savings and investment options. It is not intended to make recommendations for specific investments. Also, rules and regulations governing

Choosing an Advisor

According to the U.S. Department of Labor, financial analysts and personal financial advisors provide analysis and guidance to businesses and individuals to help them with their investment decisions. Both types of specialists gather financial information, analyze it, and make recommendations to their clients. However, their job duties differ because of the type of investment information they provide and the clients for whom they work. Financial analysts assess the economic performance of companies and industries for firms and institutions with money to invest. Personal financial advisors generally assess the financial needs of individuals, offering them a wide range of options.

Choosing someone to help us make good financial decisions is as important as the decisions we will make. So, how do you know who to use?

- Find someone who has the appropriate licenses and certifications for their business.
- Ask about fees. Everyone is paid in some way, either as a commission for what they sell you or as a fee for their services. Know up front what you are expected to pay and when.
- Retain control of your decisions. Never give your advisor the right to make decisions for you. They are there to help guide your choices, not buy and sell without your consent. Ditto for a blank contract! Only sign after you are comfortable with the terms and all documents are completed.
- Remain independent. Your advisor is your consultant, but not a business partner. Beware of any advisor who wants to become a co-owner of your investment or wants to share in your profits.
- Ask your friends for recommendations. Make an appointment with persons they recommend and interview them to determine if you can work with them. Look for someone with a good reputation, in a professional setting, who treats you and others with dignity and respect.
- Be sure they are interested in you and your future—not just your money.
- Interview more than one advisor before making a final decision.
- Continue to learn about personal finance issues. Read and stay informed on current trends, news options, and other financial issues.
- Remember, no one cares as much about your money and your future as you!!!!

investment options are subject to change. For advice on your specific situation, contact a financial planner, investment specialist, or other financial expert.)

LIVIN' LARGE: SAVING AND INVESTING

1. Be consistent when establishing a savings routine. Even small amounts will grow if you save often!
2. Diversify your savings and investments portfolio. Using a broad-based strategy for saving and investing will increase your ability to build wealth.

3. Remember your long-term goals. By keeping your focus on future wants and needs, you will be more motivated to save and less likely to make unnecessary purchases.

4. Make informed choices when choosing your investments and your financial advisors. A little investigation today may save you thousands of dollars tomorrow.

5. Tomorrow will not take care of itself. Social security and other government programs are supplemental; relying only on them for your retirement will require you to make significant changes in your lifestyle. Besides, social security and other government benefits cannot be passed along to future generations.

6. Paying yourself is just as important as paying other bills. Set up a savings routine by having money automatically transferred into a savings account each month.

7. Be sure you get all of your match from an employer. Anything less than the maximum is like throwing money away—and no one wants to do that.

8. It's okay to take a risk, but take an educated, informed risk. After all, it's your money and your future.

9. The interest rate on your savings represents the return on your money. If that return is less than the inflation rate, you are losing money each year. Rethink your savings and investing options to protect your future earnings.

10. Paying off debt as soon as possible may be your best savings plan. Continuing to pay high interest rates on credit cards will quickly erode any financial future. Work with a financial planner or counselor to minimize your debt load as soon as possible, increasing your contributions to savings and investment accounts as you reduce the amount paid to others.

The following websites are helpful in your planning:

http://www.ssa.gov/planners/calculators.htm

The government's social security website includes several different calculators, including one designed to estimate your potential benefit amounts using different retirement dates and levels of future earnings. The calculators will show your **retirement** benefits as well as **disability** and **survivor** benefit amounts on your record if you should become disabled or die today.

http://cgi.money.cnn.com/tools/retirementplanner/retirementplanner.jsp

CNN's retirement planner helps you estimate how well your savings program is preparing you for retirement. It gives you an idea of how much you will need to retire and offers suggestions for improving your financial plan.

http://www.aarp.org/money/

Visit the AARP website to use its retirement calculator and to take a tour of various type of retirement accounts currently available.

http://www.finaid.org/calculators/compoundinterest.phtml

This website offers various calculators, including one that illustrates compounding interest.

http://www.bankrate.com/brm/calc/savecalc.asp

This calculator will compute how much you have to save to reach your goal and create an individualized chart showing how much you need to save every month.

http://www.napfa.org/index2.htm

The National Association of Personal Financial Advisors has information on selecting the right financial advisor and tips for planning your financial future.

For more on choosing an advisor, complete Backstage Pass on pages 95–96.

CHAPTER TEN

MAKIN' YOUR MONEY ROCK

What comes to mind when you think of the word "millionaire"? Do you imagine lavish homes, or pulling up to a posh restaurant while you hand the valet the keys to your Porsche? If life were a music video, your perception would be correct. But in the "real world," millionaires often look just like us.

Millionaires don't always live in the richest area in the biggest house or drive the fastest car. Those who have reached that prestigious mark are usually great stewards of their finances. They didn't win the lottery or become famous; they simply planned and executed a strategy for earning and saving their money. In fact, more than 80 percent of millionaires are ordinary people who have accumulated their wealth in one generation.

Being a millionaire does not, however, equal financial independence. Even millionaires can and do go bankrupt because they are unable to manage their personal finances. Regardless of income, the secret is learning how to minimize our spending while maximizing our earnings. Those earnings include the return on our investments, not just our income—and spending includes the amount we pay in regular monthly payments, in day-to-day expenditures, and in our taxes.

The real meaning of "livin' large" is "livin' in charge"—in charge of where our money goes and where our bucks stop.

For most of us, money is easier to earn than it is to keep. Why? Because we all go to school, to college, to specialized trainings, and other formal educational settings that teach us how to develop our human capital skills that allow us to increase our potential earnings. But, few of us are ever taught how to achieve financial independence.

Growing up in a market economy where consumers rule, spending is all around us. It's very visual. Spend 30 minutes watching television and we're soon convinced we need a new car to drive to the sale at the mall before we head to the store to buy those "new and improved" food items that will eventually send us to the pharmacy to purchase some new drug that will cure all our problems. And, we can't forget to stop for some fast food on our way! Once home, we'll spend a few minutes online to pick up those things out of stock at the mall or available by auction. All paid with some kind of plastic—whether credit or debit. And that means we rarely stop to add up how much we spend in just one of those trips. Of course, we

Try This

Think of money in terms of how long it takes you to earn it. For example, if you earn $8 an hour and a new pair of shoes cost $80, that means it will take you ten hours to earn enough money to buy the shoes. Now, are those shoes really worth ten hours of your life?

know how much money we "save" with every purchase! But no mention about how much we save *without* those purchases.

Using checks, plastic, or other technology-based transaction makes money impersonal. How many of us really "see" a paycheck each month or "see" how much money we spend? Most transactions are electronic, happening way out there in cyberspace. A cashless society has become a mindless society when it comes to spending. We don't see it, so we don't even think about it how it is adding up the cost and taking away from our financial future. The blessings of living with these technological advances can become a curse, unless we develop a "take charge" attitude.

Millionaire Game

Let's play a little game. Before each statement below, put a "1" if you agree or a "2" if you disagree with the statement as to how much (or how little) you know about millionaires.

_____ 1. Most millionaires live in older homes and have lived there for 20 years or more.

_____ 2. Most millionaires are college graduates.

_____ 3. Millionaires in the United States have an average income of less than $150,000.

_____ 4. More millionaires drive Fords and Buicks than BMWs and Mercedes.

_____ 5. Most millionaires are goal-oriented.

_____ 6. Most millionaires are single, with no children.

_____ 7. Most millionaires are retired.

_____ 8. Most millionaires refuse to invest in stocks or bonds.

_____ 9. Most millionaires are athletes, entertainers, or superstars.

_____10. Most millionaires let someone else do their work.

Check out the answers at the end of this chapter to see how well you did.

And, who ever sees "savings"? After all, postponing a purchase is delaying the visual satisfaction associated with money. It takes a while to start seeing returns; but if we're faithful to our savings and financial plan, it will pay off. Few things we purchase last longer than the peace of mind that comes from living within our means.

GAMBLING

Society provides hundreds of temptations or barriers to financial success. Webster's Dictionary defines a barrier as "an obstruction such as a fence or anything that hinders or blocks your way." Overspending, addictions and other personal behaviors are potential roadblocks in our financial path.

Thorstein Veblen, a famous economist in the 19th Century, wrote extensively about "conspicuous consumption," meaning we are more concerned about appearances and accumulation of THINGS instead of accumulation of WEALTH. Today, we seem to believe that having a closet full of clothes or a room full of electronic gadgets makes us wealthy. In reality, conspicuous consumption wears down our income and swamps us with compounding debt.

The proliferation of casinos, lotteries and other gambling opportunities are also potential barriers to achieving our financial goals. For most of us, gambling is simply a form of entertainment; for others, however, it becomes an addiction that wrecks their financial lives.

Current statistics indicate that about three percent of the adult population in the United States are addicted to gambling, resulting in serious problems with debt, job loss, personal health issues, family matters and even suicide. Other studies show that teens and young adults are three times more likely than adults to become gambling addicts.

Gambler's Anonymous provides a list of 20 questions to help us determine if we have a gambling problem. Answering the following questions can help us decide if we are a compulsive gambler, or if we want to go "cold turkey" and stop.

1. Did you ever lose time from work or school due to gambling?
2. Has gambling ever made your home life unhappy?
3. Did gambling affect your reputation?
4. Have you ever felt remorse after gambling?
5. Did you ever gamble to get money with which to pay debts or otherwise solve financial difficulties?
6. Did gambling cause a decrease in your ambition or efficiency?
7. After losing did you feel you must return as soon as possible and win back your losses?
8. After a win did you have a strong urge to return and win more?

9. Did you often gamble until your last dollar was gone?

10. Did you ever borrow to finance your gambling?

11. Have you ever sold anything to finance gambling?

12. Were you reluctant to use "gambling money" for normal expenditures?

13. Did gambling make you careless of the welfare of yourself or your family?

14. Did you ever gamble longer than you had planned?

15. Have you ever gambled to escape worry or trouble?

16. Have you ever committed, or considered committing, an illegal act to finance gambling?

17. Did gambling cause you to have difficulty in sleeping?

18. Do arguments, disappointments or frustrations create within you an urge to gamble?

19. Did you ever have an urge to celebrate any good fortune by a few hours of gambling?

20. Have you ever considered self destruction or suicide as a result of your gambling?

Most compulsive gamblers will answer yes to at least seven of these questions.

Learning to recognize the roadblocks and temptations in our own lives will help stay focused on our goals or find our way back on track when we stray from them.

IT'S A WRAP

It's never too late for a "money makeover" to start our path to financial independence. Most of us don't wake up one day and just decide we want to make bad choices about our lives—or our money. But we can wake up and decide to make strategic changes that will improve our well-being. If knowledge is power, then applying what we have learned about money empowers us to make better choices.

Even with the best of plans, life happens. Knowing how to respond in times of crises and having a back-up plan will protect us from financial disaster.

LIVIN' LARGE TOP 10

1. Comparison shop. Whether buying a new vehicle, renting an apartment or purchasing a new cell phone plan, shop around for the best deal before making a decision. When comparison shopping, keep in mind that you need to compare more than just the initial cost. So, develop a criteria for what you **need** before you start shopping.

2. Minimize trendy purchases. Build your wardrobe and home design around the classics. Trends come and go—and there goes your investment. You can purchase inexpensive accessories to add the latest fad to make a fashion statement.

3. Practice maintenance. Cars, appliances, and even our bodies benefit from regular maintenance checks. Keeping your things in good running order lengthens their lifespan and saves us expensive repair or replacement costs.

4. Know the difference between wants and needs. If we can delay the purchase without sacrificing our health or our life, then it's probably a want. If we can substitute a less expensive item and receive basically the same results, then it's probably a want. Sorry, but those designer-label clothes, that new four-wheel drive truck, that slim-line photo cell phone, and those stops for designer coffee are wants not needs. Wants are spending leaks that drain your finances.

5. Practice self-control. "They" are not responsible for who you are, what you do, or how you spend your money. Regardless of the emotional appeal to spend, you are still in control. It's your life and your plan—and your goals.

6. Don't get discouraged. No one is perfect or expected to be. But once you make a bad choice or get into financial trouble, don't give up. Instead, get help and get back on your path to financial independence.

7. Talk about money with family members. Sharing the same or complementary values and feelings about money with your life mate will help ensure your family has financial success. It is also important to include children in future discussions about family goals and money management.

8. Know your "buttons." Certain feelings, emotions, or stimuli are like pushing money buttons. Learning what pushes your buttons will help keep you in control and defend against impulse spending.

9. Remember, life is a long journey. You have the potential to live over 80 years. Plan for the journey, rather than just living for today.

10. Hang out with people who are financially successful. Build a team of friends and co-workers that believe life is full of opportunities and share your values.

Bonus: Live smart. There is no substitute for financial know-how. Livin' large means you are livin' smart! Go for it!

Threatening Weather? Remember the P's

A tornado warning has been issued for your area, and you are told to take cover. What do you do? Part of being financially successful is being **Pre**pared in case of emergencies.

Experts tell us to follow the "*P*" Rule. Round up the things in your life that start with the letter "*P*"—and take cover immediately. Those "*p*" words include the following:

- *P*eople: Be sure you have a plan for your friends and family. Know when and how you will communicate during times of natural disasters or unexpected catastrophic events. Before heading to a cellar or safe room, be sure everyone is aware of your plan and how to get there. Persons who are older or younger or have health problems may need additional assistance, so include their special needs in your plans.

- *P*rescriptions: Keep your medication in a location that is easy to grab and run. You may be without power or have damage to you home, so take essential medications with you when you head for safety.

- *P*hotographs: When ordered to evacuate or take cover, take irreplaceable photographs or photo albums. If these are placed in a strategic location as part of your safety plan, they will easy to find and can be grabbed in little or no time.

- *P*ersonal records: Unplug your hard-drive and run! Most of us keep important personal information on our computers and would be lost if it were wiped out. Another option is to store everything on a flash drive . . . then grab it in a "flash" before leaving.

- *P*apers: Keep important papers (insurance policies, medical records, check book and the like) in one place so you can find them easily and take them with you.

These rules apply during times of severe weather such as tornadoes, potential flooding, hurricanes or other events related to Mother Nature. But the same is true in case of any unexpected calamity that requires us to take immediate action to protect ourselves and our families . . . and our personal finances.

For more on savvy spending, complete Backstage Pass on pages 97–100.

Answers

If you agree with the first five statements and disagree with the last five, then go to the head of the line! Are you surprised by some of the answers? Now, has your perception of millionaires changed?

Based on *The Millionaire Next Door* by Thomas J. Stanley and William D. Danko, following are some interesting characteristics of millionaires. The book was published in 1996 so the statistics may have changed somewhat, but the conclusions remain the same.

1. Most millionaires live in older homes and have lived there for 20 years or more. Moving is expensive and so are house payments! The average value of their homes is about $320,000.

2. Most millionaires are college graduates. In fact, about 80 percent are college graduates and about 40 percent have graduate degrees. Getting a college education does pay off.

3. Millionaires in the United States have an average income of less than $150,000. Stanley and Danko found the average income in 1996 was $130,000. Even adjusted for inflation, that amount has appreciated greatly. This is further proof that it's what you do with your income that matters. Living large means living on less than you can afford to spend, which pays dividends for the future. Wealth is not the same as income.

4. More millionaires drive Fords and Buicks than BMWs and Mercedes, and few of them actually drive new cars. Expensive cars equal big car payments, which consume a large percentage of our income. Driving more moderately priced cars promotes financial independence.

5. Most millionaires are goal-oriented. They set personal and financial goals, using financial planning tools such as spending plans or budgets to accomplish them. Wealth results from hard work and commitment to the future.

6. Most millionaires are married and have an average of three children. Interestingly, most remain in their first (and only) marriages and still live in their hometowns.

7. Only one in five millionaires is retired. The remainder work in a variety of professions, including doctors, lawyers, accountants, auctioneers, farmers, and construction workers. Most are entrepreneurs or self-employed.

8. Millionaires spend significantly more hours per month planning and managing investments than nonmillionaires. Nearly all the millionaires we surveyed own stocks; most have 20 percent or more of their wealth in publicly traded stocks. But they don't engage in day trading or other high-risk, short-term strategies with their stocks. They choose wisely and invest for the long run.

9. While athletes, entertainers, and superstars earn mega-incomes, few have found a way to keep it because of their spending habits and lack of investment savvy.

10. Most millionaires live rather simple lives. They invest 15 to 20 percent of their income and make many of their own investment decisions. They pay themselves first, and spend less than they can afford to spend. Most are self-made millionaires that come from humble beginnings and are modest, caring, and kind people who are socially engaged in their communities.

BACKSTAGE PASS
ACTIVITIES

Chapter 1

BACKSTAGE PASS

Setting Goals

There's no time like the present to get started thinking about your goals. The following questions will help guide you through the process:

A career goal: _____

What I must do to accomplish it: _____

The time I need to accomplish it: _____

A financial goal: _____

What I must do to accomplish it: _____

The time I need to accomplish it: _____

A personal goal: _____

What I must do to accomplish it: _____

The time I need to accomplish it: _____

A family goal: _____

What I must do to accomplish it: _____

The time I need to accomplish it: _____

An educational goal: _____

What I must do to accomplish it: _____

The time I need to accomplish it: _____

Chapter 2

BACKSTAGE PASS

Interview Questions

When going for an interview, it is important to have questions to ask the interviewer. Remember, not only are they interviewing you—you are also interviewing them to determine if this job or company is really the best fit for you. Here is an opportunity to start listing possible questions to ask a potential employer:

Question 1._____

_____

_____.

Question 2._____

_____

_____.

Question 3._____

_____

_____.

Question 4._____

_____

_____.

Question 5._____

_____

_____.

Chapter 3

BACKSTAGE PASS

Tracking Your Expenses

Use this tracking form to help you determine how much you are spending each day. It will help you adjust your spending habits to establish a successful budget or spending plan.

My Daily Expenses		
Date	Expense Description	Amount Spent

Chapter 3 Backstage Pass (*Continued*)

Spending Plans and Budgets

Here is a sample budget to help you get started. You may need to adjust some of the categories to better reflect your specific income and expenses. Complete this form after using the tracking form to determine your expenses. What changes do you need to make to ensure you have enough money to cover your monthly expenses?

My Spending Plan			
	Current Income	Income Changes	New Budget
Take home pay			
Overtime pay			
Other monthly income			
Total income			
	Current Expenses	Spending Changes	New Budget
Rent			
Renter's insurance			
Electricity			
Gas			
Water			
Telephone			
Cable TV			
Internet service			
Credit card payments			
Groceries			
Eating out			
Clothing			
Car loan			
Car insurance			
Gasoline			
Entertainment			
Tuition and books			
Miscellaneous daily expenses			
Savings			
Other expenses:			
Total expense			
Monthly net (income-expenses)			
Additional savings or investments			

Chapter 4

BACKSTAGE PASS

Computing Your Taxes

Congratulations on completing on your first year of full-time employment with the YUM Restaurant Group. You are single, with no dependents and very focused on starting your career. You began the year on the wait staff, but your hard work, education and commitment resulted in a promotion to the management training program. During the first four months, you earned a minimal salary that was supplemented with tips. Now, as part of the management training program, you are on straight salary with full benefits. The salary is good, but those taxes sure take a bite out of your monthly pay check. You have also opened a savings account to start an emergency fund, just in case something happens and you need cash immediately. April 15 is just around the corner and you need help filing your taxes. Following is a summary of your earnings and taxes for the past year. Use this information to complete the W2 and 1040EZ.

Salary—waiting tables	$1,760
Tips—waiting tables	$7,048
Salary—management training	$14,400
Federal Withholding	$2,424
State Withholding	$727
Interest Earned	$391

Following are the tax rates you are paying:

Federal Tax—15%

State Tax—4.5%

Social Security Tax—6.2%

Medicare Tax—2.9%

Form

1040EZ

Department of the Treasury—Internal Revenue Service

Income Tax Return for Single and Joint Filers With No Dependents (99) **2006**

OMB No. 1545-0074

Label

(See page 11.)

Use the IRS label.

Otherwise, please print or type.

L A B E L   H E R E

Your first name and initial	Last name

If a joint return, spouse's first name and initial	Last name

Home address (number and street). If you have a P.O. box, see page 11. | Apt. no.

City, town or post office, state, and ZIP code. If you have a foreign address, see page 11.

Your social security number

Spouse's social security number

▲ **You must enter your SSN(s) above.** ▲

Checking a box below will not change your tax or refund.

Presidential Election Campaign (page 11) ▶

Check here if you, or your spouse if a joint return, want $3 to go to this fund . . . . ▶ ☐ **You**   ☐ **Spouse**

Income

Attach Form(s) W-2 here.

Enclose, but do not attach, any payment.

1 Wages, salaries, and tips. This should be shown in box 1 of your Form(s) W-2. Attach your Form(s) W-2. | **1**

2 Taxable interest. If the total is over $1,500, you cannot use Form 1040EZ. | **2**

3 Unemployment compensation and Alaska Permanent Fund dividends (see page 13). | **3**

4 Add lines 1, 2, and 3. This is your **adjusted gross income.** | **4**

5 If someone can claim you (or your spouse if a joint return) as a dependent, check the applicable box(es) below and enter the amount from the worksheet on back.

☐ **You**   ☐ **Spouse**

If no one can claim you (or your spouse if a joint return), enter $8,450 if **single;** $16,900 if **married filing jointly.** See back for explanation. | **5**

6 Subtract line 5 from line 4. If line 5 is larger than line 4, enter -0-. This is your **taxable income.** ▶ | **6**

Payments and tax

7 Federal income tax withheld from box 2 of your Form(s) W-2. | **7**

8a Earned income credit (EIC). | **8a**

b Nontaxable combat pay election. | 8b

9 Credit for federal telephone excise tax paid. Attach Form 8913 if required. | **9**

10 Add lines 7, 8a, and 9. These are your **total payments.** ▶ | **10**

11 **Tax.** Use the amount on **line 6 above** to find your tax in the tax table on pages 24–32 of the booklet. Then, enter the tax from the table on this line. | **11**

Refund

Have it directly deposited! See page 18 and fill in 12b, 12c, and 12d or Form 8888.

12a If line 10 is larger than line 11, subtract line 11 from line 10. This is your **refund.** If Form 8888 is attached, check here ▶ ☐ | **12a**

▶ **b** Routing number | ▶ **c** Type: ☐ Checking ☐ Savings

▶ **d** Account number

Amount you owe

13 If line 11 is larger than line 10, subtract line 10 from line 11. This is the **amount you owe.** For details on how to pay, see page 19. ▶ | **13**

Third party designee

Do you want to allow another person to discuss this return with the IRS (see page 20)? ☐ **Yes.** Complete the following. ☐ **No**

Designee's name ▶ | Phone no. ▶ ( ) | Personal identification number (PIN)

Sign here

Joint return? See page 11.

Keep a copy for your records.

Under penalties of perjury, I declare that I have examined this return, and to the best of my knowledge and belief, it is true, correct, and accurately lists all amounts and sources of income I received during the tax year. Declaration of preparer (other than the taxpayer) is based on all information of which the preparer has any knowledge.

Your signature	Date	Your occupation	Daytime phone number ( )
Spouse's signature. If a joint return, **both** must sign.	Date	Spouse's occupation	

Paid preparer's use only

Preparer's signature ▶		Date	Check if self-employed ☐	Preparer's SSN or PTIN
Firm's name (or yours if self-employed), address, and ZIP code			EIN	
			Phone no. ( )	

For Disclosure, Privacy Act, and Paperwork Reduction Act Notice, see page 22.

Cat. No. 11329W

Form **1040EZ** (2006)

Use this form if

- Your filing status is single or married filing jointly. If you are not sure about your filing status, see page 11.
- You (and your spouse if married filing jointly) were under age 65 and not blind at the end of 2006. If you were born on January 1, 1942, you are considered to be age 65 at the end of 2006.
- You do not claim any dependents. For information on dependents, use TeleTax topic 354 (see page 6).
- Your taxable income (line 6) is less than $100,000.
- You do not claim any adjustments to income. For information on adjustments to income, use TeleTax topics 451-453, 455, and 456 (see page 6).
- The only tax credits you can claim are the earned income credit and the credit for the federal telephone excise tax. For information on credits, use TeleTax topics 601-608 and 610 (see page 6).
- You had only wages, salaries, tips, taxable scholarship or fellowship grants, unemployment compensation, or Alaska Permanent Fund dividends, and your taxable interest was not over $1,500. But if you earned tips, including allocated tips, that are not included in box 5 and box 7 of your Form W-2, you may not be able to use Form 1040EZ (see page 12). If you are planning to use Form 1040EZ for a child who received Alaska Permanent Fund dividends, see page 13.
- You did not receive any advance earned income credit payments. If you cannot use this form, use TeleTax topic 352 (see page 6).

Filling in your return

If you received a scholarship or fellowship grant or tax-exempt interest income, such as on municipal bonds, see the booklet before filling in the form. Also, see the booklet if you received a Form 1099-INT showing federal income tax withheld or if federal income tax was withheld from your unemployment compensation or Alaska Permanent Fund dividends.

For tips on how to avoid common mistakes, see page 20.

Remember, you must report all wages, salaries, and tips even if you do not get a Form W-2 from your employer. You must also report all your taxable interest, including interest from banks, savings and loans, credit unions, etc., even if you do not get a Form 1099-INT.

Worksheet for dependents who checked one or both boxes on line 5

(keep a copy for your records)

Use this worksheet to figure the amount to enter on line 5 if someone can claim you (or your spouse if married filing jointly) as a dependent, even if that person chooses not to do so. To find out if someone can claim you as a dependent, use TeleTax topic 354 (see page 6).

A. Amount, if any, from line 1 on front . _____

                       +   300.00   Enter total ▶   A. _____

B. Minimum standard deduction . . . . B. ____850.00____

C. Enter the **larger** of line A or line B here . . . . C. _____

D. Maximum standard deduction. If **single,** enter $5,150; if **married filing jointly,** enter $10,300 . . . . D. _____

E. Enter the **smaller** of line C or line D here. This is your standard deduction   E. _____

F. Exemption amount.
- If single, enter -0-.
- If married filing jointly and—   F. _____

    —both you and your spouse can be claimed as dependents, enter -0-.

    —only one of you can be claimed as a dependent, enter $3,300.

G. Add lines E and F. Enter the total here and on line 5 on the front . . . G. _____

If you did not check any boxes on line 5, enter on line 5 the amount shown below that applies to you.

- Single, enter $8,450. This is the total of your standard deduction ($5,150) and your exemption ($3,300).
- Married filing jointly, enter $16,900. This is the total of your standard deduction ($10,300), your exemption ($3,300), and your spouse's exemption ($3,300).

Mailing return

Mail your return by **April 16, 2007.** If you live in Maine, Maryland, Massachusetts, New Hampshire, New York, Vermont, or the District of Columbia, you have until April 17, 2007. Use the envelope that came with your booklet. If you do not have that envelope or if you moved during the year, see the back cover for the address to use.

 Printed on recycled paper

Form **1040EZ** (2006)

	a Employee's social security number				
		OMB No. 1545-0008	Safe, accurate, FAST! Use	IRS *e-file*	Visit the IRS website at *www.irs.gov/efile*.

b Employer identification number (EIN)	**1** Wages, tips, other compensation	**2** Federal income tax withheld
c Employer's name, address, and ZIP code	**3** Social security wages	**4** Social security tax withheld
	5 Medicare wages and tips	**6** Medicare tax withheld
	7 Social security tips	**8** Allocated tips
d Control number	**9** Advance EIC payment	**10** Dependent care benefits

e Employee's first name and initial Last name Suff.	**11** Nonqualified plans	**12a** See instructions for box 12
	13 Statutory employee Retirement plan Third-party sick pay	**12b**
	14 Other	**12c**
		12d
f Employee's address and ZIP code		

15 State Employer's state ID number	**16** State wages, tips, etc.	**17** State income tax	**18** Local wages, tips, etc.	**19** Local income tax	**20** Locality name

Form **W-2** Wage and Tax Statement   **2007**   Department of the Treasury—Internal Revenue Service

Copy B—To Be Filed With Employee's **FEDERAL** Tax Return.
This information is being furnished to the Internal Revenue Service.

Chapter 5

BACKSTAGE PASS

Choosing a Credit Card

Not all credit cards are the same. In fact, they vary greatly. Before taking out a credit card, think about how you will use it. Do you expect to pay your monthly bill in full? Carry over a balance from month to month? Use it for cash advances? Use it only for emergencies?

The answers to these questions will help you choose the best card for your needs.

Use the following checklist to compare three different cards. Information about most of these features is listed in the disclosure box that must appear in all printed credit card solicitations and applications.

Comparing Credit Cards

Features	Card A	Card B	Card C
What is the APR (annual percentage rate of interest) on each card for the following?			
Purchases?	_____	_____	_____
Cash advances?	_____	_____	_____
Balance transfers?	_____	_____	_____
If you are late with a payment, does the APR increase?	_____	_____	_____
If so, to what rate?	_____	_____	_____
How long is the grace period			
If you carry over a balance?	_____	_____	_____
If you pay off the balance each month?	_____	_____	_____
For cash advances?	_____	_____	_____
What are the fees?			
Annual?	_____	_____	_____
Late payments?	_____	_____	_____
Over the credit line?	_____	_____	_____
Set up?	_____	_____	_____
What are the cash advance features?			
Transaction fees?	_____	_____	_____
Limits?	_____	_____	_____
How much is the credit limit?	_____	_____	_____
What kind of card is it?	_____	_____	_____
Secured, Regular, or Premium			
Does the card have other features?	_____	_____	_____
Rebates	_____	_____	_____
Frequent flyer miles	_____	_____	_____
Insurance	_____	_____	_____
Other	_____	_____	_____

Based on a comparison chart available at *http://www.federalreserve.gov/pubs/shop/checklist.htm*

Chapter 6

BACKSTAGE PASS

Skimmin' and Schemin'

Ever felt like you were on a PHISHING expedition when you download your email?

Millions of dollars in transactions each year are fraudulent. While most business today is completely legal, there are a growing number of people who want an easy buck at your expense. Oftentimes, people trying to pull a fast one on us are simply appealing to our desire to make a truckload of money overnight—with little, if any, effort. But, Grandma's rule is still true: If it sounds too good to be true, then it probably is!

Following are some common scams and schemes:

Identify Theft: Someone steals your name, Social Security number, credit card number or some other form of personal identification and uses that information to get credit cards, open charge accounts, open checking accounts and write hot checks—all in your name.

Credit Repair: Someone contacts you offering to help clean up your credit report and raise your credit scare. They may have a way to erase bankruptcy or bad credit history from your report—for a small fee.

College Financial Aid: A company advertises that millions of dollars in scholarships go unclaimed every year. And, for a small fee, they guarantee to find you scholarship money to attend college. If not, they will return your fee.

Pyramid: With a pyramid, the first participants receive payments for recruiting additional members. The problem is this: there are not enough people to keep the pyramid growing steadily to ensure you get anything from your "investment." Such schemes may come as games, buying clubs, chain letters, mail order sales, birthday clubs or other multi-level businesses.

Ponzi: Someone offers you an investment opportunity, promising much higher financial returns or dividends than from traditional investments. All the time, he is probably planning to take the money and run—once he has involved enough people to make it worthwhile.

419 Letter: You receive a letter or email from someone in another country wanting help to transfer money illegally out of their country, and they need YOUR help. In return for your personal information (bank account number of other information), they will share the transferred money with you.

Internet: You receive an email from "your" bank saying they need to confirm your account number . . . so please send it back to them to ensure they are providing the correct services for you. Or, you get an email from the IRS asking for your bank account or SSN so they can transfer funds for you. Or, you get an email making you the offer of a lifetime for a special purchase. These types of Internet schemes are frequently called Phishing

Schemes, Scams, and ID Theft

Identity Theft	Credit Repair	College Financial Aid	Pyramid	419 Letter	Ponzi	Phishing

Use these terms to identify the different types of fraudulent activities described below:

Their Pitch | **Your Hit**

You receive a phone call from a bill collector who says you are six months behind in credit card payments. You explain that you don't have an account with them, even though they have your name, your phone number and your address.

_____

You receive the following letter in the mail: Did you know that thousands of dollars in college scholarships were not claimed last year? For only $99, we can guarantee you at least $10,000 in scholarship funds—or return your payment.

_____

The following email arrives: We have suffered a breach in security and need your account number to verify the amount of money in your checking account. Please send that information to us as soon as possible to ensure you have immediate access to your funds.

_____

Your friend calls and invites you to a meeting at the local library. He has been in touch with a man who promises to triple your money! If you will invest $5,000 tonight, you will have $15,000 in just four months. How can you beat that deal???

_____

You are looking for a job to help pay for your college expenses. It costs only $100 to get started in your own business. And, if you will recruit more people to work for you, you can keep part of their $100, plus make a percentage of their sales.

_____

Chapter 7

BACKSTAGE PASS

Apartment Hunting

Finding an apartment can be overwhelming. Use the following Apartment Hunting Checklist to compare three rental options before making a final decision. You may want to develop a similar checklist when selecting a home to purchase.

Apartment Hunting Checklist

	Apartment A	Apartment B	Apartment C
1. Is the complex well maintained?			
2. Is it close to my work place or school?			
3. Is the neighborhood safe?			
4. Is it close to stores, banks, and other services we use?			
5. Is it close to public transportation?			
6. Do the average monthly utilities fit into my budget?			
7. Is there adequate parking for my car?			
8. Does the apartment include the amenities I like to use?			
9. Did someone recommend this area or complex to me?			

House Hunting Checklist

	House A	House B	House C
1. Is the neighborhood well maintained?			
2. Is it close to my work place or school?			
3. Is the neighborhood safe?			
4. Is it close to stores, banks, and other services we use?			
5. Is it close to public transportation?			
6. Do the average monthly utilities fit into my budget?			
7. Is there adequate parking for my car or for my family and friends?			
8. Does the apartment include the amenities I like to use?			
9. Did someone recommend this area to me?			

Chapter 8

BACKSTAGE PASS

Insurance

PART ONE

1. List ten possible risks that you face in a typical week. What steps are you taking to protect yourself from those risks?

Possible Risks   Risk Management

_____   _____

_____   _____

_____   _____

_____   _____

_____   _____

_____   _____

_____   _____

_____   _____

_____   _____

_____   _____

2. For which of the above risks should you purchase insurance to minimize your potential losses? Why?

PART TWO

Type of Insurance	Terms	Potential Loss
Auto	You can purchase auto insurance with a $1,000 deductible for $200 per month.	The average accident in your city costs $2,000 in repairs, but could escalate to $500,000 per person if you are found liable to injuries to others. Because you drive 80 miles round trip to work each day in a high traffic city, there is a 35% probability that you will be involved in an accident this year.
Health	You can purchase health insurance through your company for $100 per month that covers major medical expenses.	Persons your age in your area spend an average of $1,800 annually on doctor visits and medication, but that average jumps to $300,000 if hospitalized for a week. Costs could rapidly increase if diagnosed with a major illness. Chances are good that you will have some medical need during the year, but only slim that you will require hospitalization.

Cancer	You can purchase an additional cancer insurance policy through your company for $20 per month that will supplement your health insurance policy in case you are diagnosed with any form of cancer.	You have no history of cancer in your family but are worried about "the big C." You've seen what happened to others who had cancer! Because of your lifestyle and your family history, chances are less than 1% that you will have this disease.
Disability	You can purchase a basic disability package at work for $35 per month. This policy will provide 60% of your income if you are off work for more than 30 days, due to an illness.	You work in an office as an accountant, but are often required to travel on the job. You like to play basketball in the evening with friends at the gym and go snowskiing two or three times each winter. You are also on the company's softball team. Because you engage in some medium to high risk sporting activities, you have a 25% chance of incurring an injury. Otherwise, you have no major health problems and eat a healthy diet.
Renter's	You can purchase renter's insurance for $25 per month.	You are currently renting an apartment in one of the best complexes in the city. Your apartment has a security system, smoke detectors and a sprinkler system. Because you are a young professional, you have just bought your first new sofa and bedroom set. You feel safe and have a less than 10% chance of suffering a loss.
Life	Your company provides you with $20,000 in life insurance, but you can purchase a $100,000 policy for an additional $15 per month.	You are single and have no dependents.
Long-term care	You can purchase a long-term care policy at work for $25 per month.	You have just graduated from college, age 23 and in good health.

A. Based on the information provided above, which types of insurance would you purchase? What is the total monthly cost of your decision?

B. Suppose you can only afford to spend $4,000 annually (about $330 per month) on insurance premiums. What changes would you make in your insurance purchases?

C. Suppose you were married and had young children. How would this impact your previous choices?

Chapter 9

BACKSTAGE PASS

Finding a Financial Advisor

With the increase in self-directed retirement plans and investment options, more people are seeking the assistance of a financial advisor. Following is a checklist to help you make an informed decision when selecting someone to advise you on your financial matters.

Planner's Name _____

Company _____

Address _____

Phone _____

Date _____

1. Do you have experience in providing advice on the topics below? If yes, indicate the number of years.
   - Retirement plannning
   - Investment planning
   - Tax planning
   - Estate planning
   - Insurance planning
   - Integrated planning
   - Other

2. What are your areas of specialization?

   What qualifies you in this field?

3a. How long have you been offering financial planning advice to clients?
   - Less than 1 year
   - 1 to 4 years
   - 5 to ten years
   - More than ten years

3b. How many clients do you currently have?
   - Less than 10 clients.
   - 10 to 39
   - 40 to 79
   - 80+

4. Briefly describe your work history.

5. What are your educational qualifications? Give area of study.
   - Certificate
   - Undergraduate degree
   - Advanced degree
   - Other

6. What financial planning designation(s) or certification(s) do you hold?
   - Certified Financial Planner™ or CFP®
   - Certified Public Accountant/Personal Financial Specialist (CPA/PFS)
   - Chartered Financial Consultant (ChFC)
   - Other

7. What financial planning continuing education requirements do you fulfill?

8. What licenses do you hold?
   - Insurance
   - Securities
   - CPA
   - J.D.
   - Other

9a. Are you personally licensed or registered as an Investment Advisor with the:
   - State(s)?
   - Federal government?

   If no, why not?

9b. Is your firm licensed or registered as an Investment Advisor with the:

- State(s)?
- Federal government?

If no, why not?

9c. Will you provide me with your disclosure document Form ADV Part II or its state equivalent?

- Yes
- No

If no, why not?

10. What services do you offer?

11. Describe your approach to financial planning.

12a. Who will work with me?

- Planner
- Associate(s)

12b. Will the same individual(s) review my financial situation?

- Yes
- No

If no, who will?

13. How are you paid for your services?

- Fee
- Commission
- Fee and commission
- Salary
- Other

14. What do you typically charge?

   a. Fee:

     Hourly rate $ _____

     Flat fee (range) $ _____ to $ _____

     Percentage of assets under management _____ percent

   b. Commission:

     What is the approximate percentage of the investment or premium you receive on:

     stocks and bonds _____

     mutual funds _____

     annuities _____

     insurance products _____

     other _____

15a. Do you have a business affiliation with any company whose products or services you are recommending?

- Yes
- No

Explain:

   b. Is any of your compensation based on selling products?

- Yes
- No

Explain:

   c. Do professionals and sales agents to whom you may refer me send business, fees, or any other benefits to you?

- Yes
- No

Explain:

   d. Do you have an affiliation with a broker/dealer?

- Yes
- No

   e. Are you an owner of, or connected with, any other company whose services or products I will use?

- Yes
- No

Explain:

16. Do you provide a written client engagement agreement?

- Yes
- No

If no, why not?

Source: *http://www.pueblo.gsa.gov/cic_text/money/ financial-planner/10questions.html.*

Chapter 10

BACKSTAGE PASS

Savvy Spending Quiz
from moneycentral.msn.com

1. When planning your annual vacation, you:

    ○ Wait until the last minute and inevitably feel that you've spent too much and that it wasn't really worth it.

    ○ Always mean to take a vacation, but when the time comes, you usually decide you can't spare the money.

    ○ Use money set aside in your budget for leisure.

    ○ Go "all out," reasoning that your job is stressful and you need the relaxation, no matter what the cost.

2. When you receive your paycheck, you:

    ○ Have money skimmed off the top for your 401(k) plan and various pre-tax spending accounts for medical and dependent care. You then put money in regular savings and college accounts for the kids. What's left is allocated among your budget items, with discretionary items like entertainment at the bottom.

    ○ Pay off all the bills that have been piling up since your last paycheck and find there's nothing left.

    ○ Go on a shopping spree; you'll pay the bills later.

    ○ Put it all in savings.

3. When your favorite sports equipment (computer equipment, audiophile equipment) store announces a going-out-of business sale, you:

    ○ Call to check the credit limits on all your cards and get in line early the first day of the sale. You plan to spend big.

    ○ Check your mental list of equipment you were planning to buy over the next year and decide what you will buy now.

    ○ Stay home. You don't trust yourself at sales.

    ○ Buy your dream equipment; you'll skip your vacation this year.

4. Which of the following offers the highest interest rates?

    ○ Treasury bills.

    ○ Money market mutual fund.

    ○ Bank certificates of deposit.

    ○ Bank money market account.

5. What is the highest interest rate you pay on a credit card?

    ○ You take what you can get.

    ○ 18 percent.

    ○ 5.9 percent, because you switch cards to the lowest introductory rate every few months.

    ○ 10 percent, but it doesn't matter because you pay off your credit bills each month.

6. Which best describes the way you make purchases?

   ○ You've noticed a pattern of spending when you're happy or spending when you're sad.

   ○ Sometimes you worry that you don't have the same things as your friends and then you spend to catch up.

   ○ You spend in cycles, running up credit card debt and then paying it down.

   ○ You budget for your spending, allowing for a few extravagances along the way, but generally buy only what is on your list.

7. What portion of your income do you save? Include retirement plans, college accounts, an emergency fund and regular savings.

   ○ 10 to 15 percent.

   ○ Nothing.

   ○ 2 to 3 percent.

   ○ 50 percent.

8. Add up all your debt—home mortgage, second home, cars, credit cards. Don't include items such as food or utilities. What percent of your monthly income does it represent?

   ○ 35 percent or less.

   ○ 50 percent.

   ○ Not sure.

   ○ About 40 percent.

9. When you get a raise, you typically:

   ○ Don't notice.

   ○ Go on a shopping spree.

   ○ Promise yourself again that you will draw up a budget.

   ○ Treat yourself to dinner out or some item you've been wanting and then allocate the rest to savings.

10. When you think about your financial situation, you feel:

    ○ Hopeless. It seems that you keep falling further behind.

    ○ Optimistic. You're buying lots of things and soon you'll be able to start saving.

    ○ Confident. You're meeting the targets you've set for yourself.

    ○ You think about it only late at night when you can't sleep.

11. A friend calls to tell you about a once-in-a-lifetime ski weekend. You have nothing set aside for such a trip. You:

    ○ Decline and promise yourself that you'll start a ski fund.

    ○ Review your credit card balances and try to get enough money from cash advances.

    ○ Accept. You'll figure out the details later.

    ○ Decide to take a loan from your 401(k), your dad, your girlfriend. You've got to go!

12. It's holiday time. You:

    ○ Pull out your budget from last year and inflate it by the consumer price index or the size of your last salary increase.

    ○ Vow that you won't overspend by as much as you did last year.

    ○ Apply for two more credit cards.

    ○ Get drunk. You're still paying for the 2000 holiday and your cards are charged to the limit.

13. When the monthly bills come in, you:

    - ○ Don't even notice. You have arranged for automatic bill paying at the bank.
    - ○ Pay the minimum on each one and throw it in the trash.
    - ○ Put them off until the second notice and then pay the minimum.
    - ○ Pay them once a month.

14. You get a pink slip at work. You:

    - ○ Arrange for continued medical benefits from your company and, while worried, you at least pat yourself on the back for accumulating money in your emergency fund.
    - ○ Try to arrange for higher credit limits and a home equity loan.
    - ○ Plan the vacation you haven't had time for.
    - ○ Go on a shopping spree to cheer yourself up.

15. You've just been recruited for your first job after college. You:

    - ○ Draw up a budget and arrange to save 10 percent of your salary.
    - ○ Decline to sign up for the company's 401(k) plan; retirement is a long way away.
    - ○ Borrow from your parents to buy a smashing work wardrobe and a new car.
    - ○ Arrange for lines of credit.

16. You're expecting your first baby. You:

    - ○ Draw up a new budget.
    - ○ Buy a bigger house.
    - ○ Treat yourself to a last super vacation as a couple.
    - ○ Feel depressed; you're not financially successful enough to be a parent.

17. Which investment portfolio is likely to earn the best return over 10 years?

    - ○ 85 percent stocks, 15 percent bonds.
    - ○ 100 percent bank certificates of deposit.
    - ○ 50 percent stocks, 50 percent bonds.
    - ○ 40 percent stocks, 30 percent bonds, 30 percent Treasury bills.

18. You've just received a $100,000 inheritance. You:

    - ○ Adjust your portfolio of stocks and bonds, making it slightly more conservative. You don't need to take so many risks now that you have more capital.
    - ○ Feel anxious. Dad didn't really enjoy his life because he was always scrimping and saving to leave that money to you.
    - ○ Quit your job and start the business you've been dreaming about.
    - ○ Go on a trip around the world.

19. You're shopping for a home. You:

    - ○ Go for broke; you'll grow into the payments.
    - ○ Decide how much house you can afford before you shop and stick with it.
    - ○ You've been shopping for years, but you can't bring yourself to make such a big commitment.
    - ○ Realize you'll never own a home because your credit rating is too seriously impaired.

20. When you make a large purchase, you typically feel:

- ○ Elated, then let down.
- ○ Satisfied. You did your research and planned for it.
- ○ Depressed. You really don't deserve anything that costs so much.
- ○ Regretful. You probably didn't make the right decision.

http://moneycentral.msn.com/investor/calcs/n_spend/main.asp

ANSWERS

The correct answers are listed below for the questions you missed.

Question 1:
Correct Answer: You take vacations with money set aside in a separate account for leisure.

Question 2:
Correct Answer: When you receive your paycheck you have money skimmed off the top for your 401(k) plan and various pre-tax spending accounts for medical and dependent care. You then put money in regular savings and college accounts for the kids. What's left is allocated among your budget items, with discretionary items, such as entertainment, at the bottom.

Question 3:
Correct Answer: Before you go to the sports store and spend, you think about what equipment you were planning to buy over the next year.

Question 4:
Correct Answer: Treasury bills, for the most part, offer the highest rate of return of the investment options offered.

Question 5:.
Correct Answer: The best credit card strategy is one in which the rate is irrelevant because you pay the bill in full each month.

Question 6:
Correct Answer: Ideally, you rarely make "impulse purchases." Instead, you've mapped out what you're going to buy in advance.

Question 7:
Correct Answer: If you're saving 10 percent to 15 percent of your net pay each month, you're doing great. If you're saving 50 percent or more, that's incredible.

Question 8:
Correct Answer: Your debt ratio should be about 35 percent or less if you want to keep your finances under control.

Question 9:.
Correct Answer: Go ahead and have that celebratory dinner. You earned it. But then readjust your budget and try to save a little bit more with your new higher income.

Question 10:
Correct Answer: If you know you're meeting your objectives, you should feel confident. Optimism can breed unnecessary spending and a doom-and-gloom attitude won't help you figure a way out.

Question 11:
Correct Answer: Yes, it's painful to turn down that getaway weekend. But if you don't have the money, just say no.

Question 12:
Correct Answer: Keep your holiday expenditures on a budget just like you do the rest of your expenses. Otherwise, you'll be paying and paying and paying..

Question 13:
Correct Answer: If you've set up your budget properly, your bills are already factored into your account and many of them are paid seamlessly.

Question 14:
Correct Answer: Getting laid off from work is never good news, but you need to anticipate the worst. If you have, you can sanely go about the task of finding new employment without undue pressure or financial worries.

Question 15:
Correct Answer: When you get that first job, draw up your first budget. Saving early and often pays big rewards.

Question 16: You didn't select anything.

Correct Answer: A new child changes a family's budget dramatically. Adjust accordingly.

Question 17:
Correct Answer: Over the long term, stocks are your best investment bet. If you're saving for several years out, put as much as you comfortably can into stocks.

Question 18:
Correct Answer: The additional funds from an inheritance give you the luxury of becoming a bit more conservative in your investment strategy.

Question 19:
Correct Answer: It's tough to stay in a budget when you're shopping for a home, but if you don't, you could be house-rich and cash poor. Not a good combination.

Question 20:
Correct Answer: If you've planned, saved and researched for that new house or car, be content. You've done well for yourself.